MW01656970

Beauty that Grows in the Dark

Sondra Huggins

Beauty that Grows in the Dark

Sondra Huggins

International Standard Book Number
ISBN: 9798340669476

Independently published

Printed in the United States

Dedication

I want to dedicate this book to all of the women that are going through addiction and abuse and are feeling like there's no way out and nowhere to turn. Know that you can make it. It is not too late. The same God that brought me through and brought me out is able to bring you out of every circumstance. There is nothing too hard for the Lord to deliver you out from.

Thank you to my family for supporting me through this endeavor. I love and appreciate you.

Special thanks to two ladies that pushed me continually to birth this book out. Thank you Shanikua and Erica. I could not have done it without your push and prayers.

Thank you to my Spiritual Mother Pastor Tonya Williams for always praying and encouraging me through all things.

Contents

Introduction

It is my hope that my story will bring hope and encouragement to those that find themselves in a situation that they feel their life will never get better. Although life takes many of us down a path that does not appear to be working out for our good, know that the Lord has everything in control. It is not too late for you. Each of us has the capability to achieve all that we desire in life and regardless how bleak life may look. know you can overcome whatever obstacles that are in your way. My life is a living testimony of the Lord Jesus' transforming power.I have shared my story as a beacon of light for someone that may find themselves in a dark place, for someone that feels that life will never get better.There's nothing too hard for God to fix. If God did it for me; He can do it for anyone.

Chapter One

The Start to My End

I always knew that there was a calling on my life, that there was something different, something unique and special about me. There was something different that separated me from the crowd that I found myself always hanging with. I knew that there was something great down on the inside of me but I just didn't know exactly what it was. I didn't recognize the God giving gifts that were placed on the inside of me because I didn't have a true encounter with God not until later on in life as an adult. I grew up knowing about Jesus but not in the capacity that I know him today. I was raised by my mother in a single-family home and like so many families today, I was also absent of a father figure. I can remember my mother always doing the very best she could for my older sister and myself, we didn't have everything that we wanted growing up but we always had what we needed. I watched my mother work her way off of public assistance and into the workforce to provide for us. This was a quality in my mother that I loved because it showed me how strong women are and the depths a mother will go to in order to provide for their children. It also showed how strong women can be if they are determined to succeed at something in life. I inherited this quality from my mother. Through all of my life struggles and experiences I have learned that I am a strong African American woman. I hold firm to the Bible Scripture verse Philippians 4:13"I can do all things through Christ who strengthens me"(KJV) There have been many times in my life that I hit rock bottom, but I always seemed to fight my way out of it.

Growing up on my own at such a young age, I had to learn most lessons the hard way. I did not have anyone to guide me or show me the way without having ulterior motives. So I learned both the good and the bad through hard life experiences, each one shaping me in different ways and teaching me valuable lessons along the way. As a young girl I always thought about how I would grow up having this wonderful childhood full of love, fun, family, and friends getting married, having children and living in a beautiful house with the white picket fence as most young girls dream about for their future. The possibility of my life being full of darkness and pain due to drugs, prostitution, rapes and prison never entered my mind but at the young age of fifteen I was quickly thrust into the street life full of darkness, hurt and pain. The thoughts I had as a young girl of love and happiness were quickly shattered, and life began to get real fast and quick.

Being raised without a father played a major role in my life. I can see how the void of a father's presence can affect some young girls in the path that they initially take in life. For me it was something that led me to seeking love in all of the wrong places. It's not that I didn't have a father; I did, and he loved me deeply. He loved me the best way he knew how. My father battled alcohol and drug addiction, and while I know he wanted to be more present in my life and be the best dad he could, his own struggles prevented him from fully being there. I accepted that at a young age and loved him very much in spite of his shortcomings. There was a time that my father and I experienced doing drugs together. This is something no child wants to experience and during that time felt sad for my father but I also had anger towards him because he was supposed to be the protector. The one that would help me to get my life together but instead he was in the same predicament as myself. Seeing my father getting high hurt me tremendously. The love a daughter has for her parents is incomparable.

One thing I have learned over the years is that when the calling of God is on your life the enemy will try to destroy you at a young age. He will try to rob you of your purpose and destiny in God. The Scripture says in John 10:10 "The thief comes only to steal and kill and destroy. I came that they may have life and have it abundantly." (ESV)

I began to cause my mother some trouble at home, cutting school, staying out late, drinking and smoking weed experimenting in things I had no business. I found myself following the wrong crowd and indulging in things that at the time seemed harmless but, in all reality, they were leading me to destruction. I began to stay out overnight scared to go home because I knew that I had missed curfew and that I was going to get a beating and so I would just stay out for several days.

Eventually this became a negative pattern for me. I began staying out more frequently, leading my mother to call the police and reporting me as a runaway or missing child. I eventually became a ward of the court due to my mother's numerous phone calls to the police and reporting me as a runaway child. I was sent on numerous occasions to different run-away homes between the age of twelve and fourteen. This caused a strain on the family, mainly my mother. I think that our relationship became strenuous at that time because of all the times I had run away. We became distant, I knew that she loved me but simply did not know how to understand or reach me at that time in my life. At some point I picked up a spirit of rejection. I began to feel that my mother loved my sister more than she loved me, that she favored her more than me. I felt rejected. The Bible says in 1 Peter 5:8 Be sober-minded; be watchful. Your adversary the devil prowls around like a roaring lion, seeking someone to devour. (ESV) This is exactly what was happening to me. I was too young to be self-controlled and alert and the enemy came into my circumstance, placed this feeling of rejection upon me with one goal in mind and that was to destroy my young life. The Miriam Webster dictionary defines rejection as such: "to refuse to accept or believe something or someone, to turn away by not accepting." Not only did I feel rejected, but I also felt abandoned because I was no longer at home but living in a runaway home with total strangers.

At the time, I didn't recognize the role I played in everything; I was too consumed by my own emotions. I struggled deeply with feelings of abandonment and rejection because my father wasn't present in my life. This led me to stay out more often, causing my mother to call the police and report me as a runaway or missing child. The belief that my mother loved my sister more affected my decisions as a teenager. But it wasn't really about whether she favored my sister—I know now that she loved me in the best way she knew how. Still, this impacted me far more deeply than I realized at the time.

The important thing to look at here is how the enemy will take a feeling and illuminate that particular feeling causing one to become bound by it. I stayed in several runaway homes for some time but eventually got the chance to go back home. Not only would I present the same behaviors but I would end up being sent right back by the courts because the feelings that would subside for a few days would eventually pick back up and cause me to feel what I felt the first few times that made me run away. This went on for some time until one day I went home for good. Shortly after being at home with my mother and sister, my mom decided to move to Oneonta which is in upstate NY. We lived there for a short time and while there I can't say that my behavior got any better. I met a guy who was of course older, I was fourteen and he was eighteen. He was in college but originally from Brooklyn. I remember that even though I acted like I was grown, I was still just a kid.

I can remember the time I skipped school to go visit this young man at the college that he attended. This is where I learned that I was indeed not grown because he began asking me what did I want do and in my mind I just wanted to hang out and kiss and do what young people my age did back then but because I was not bold enough to say what I felt I simply said "whatever you want to do" and just like that I lost my virginity at the age of fourteen, not because I loved him, not because I wanted to but because I didn't at that time know how to speak up and simply say no.

I share this because I want every young girl or woman reading to realize that saying no is not only okay, but it also holds incredible power. As women young and old we should never be uncomfortable with the word no in any type of environment regardless of if it displeases someone else. Oftentimes as women we give of our most intimate self for all the wrong reasons. It is important that we put ourselves-first in regard to our happiness, wholeness and wellbeing. As women we must always be able to express our true feelings and speak our truth. This is something I have learned over the years, if I would have known this back then I would have made different choices, choices that would have benefitted my mental and emotional state which would have changed the course of my future.

After losing my virginity I was off for the races. I began to skip school a lot more in order to spend time with this college boy. I thought I was in love with him. The school system and legal system in upstate New York was very much different from New York City; they were much stricter to say the least. One day they called my mother to the school to meet with her because I was skipping school so much and they had my mother sign some papers which was called a pins petition. To my mother's understanding by signing the petition it would help me to stop skipping school and get me back on the right track. But like any other paperwork there is always the fine print that most people fail to read. What my mother didn't realize is that the paper work stated that if I was to break the contract and skip school again, I would become a ward of the court and they would take me out of my mother's home and place me in a group home until I turned eighteen and there would be absolutely nothing she could do, in other words she would have given up her rights and the state would have full control. Of course, not understanding the severity of the matter, I decided to continue to cut school, thinking I was grown, running after this college boy that really didn't care about my life at all. The school informed my mother that they were going to send me away to a home because I broke the signed agreement. It was then that I believe that my mother came to herself and processed what she had unintentionally done and decided to send me to live with my Aunt Sue in Inwood, New York. This was an act of desperation for my mother. She didn't want me to go and live with my aunt but the other alternative was to surrender me to the state and have me become a ward of the court. What I remember was that it was a Friday when this happened and they were going to take me on the Monday. I was terrified, it was a cold rainy morning and I can remember feeling sad and nervous; I did not understand totally why I had to be sent away and why she was putting me on this bus all by myself. I was only fifteen years old and anything could have happened to me. I was leaving my sister behind and now having to live with my aunt so far away from her. I wasn't ready for the change that was coming. My mother sent me on a bus by myself to my aunt's house on that Saturday morning. This shows the love of a mother, even though we were going through struggles she was not about to let the state take her baby girl. My mother had exhausted all other options thus the only thing she knew to do at that point was to put me on the bus to my family.

My mother was hoping that she could knock some sense into me and help get my life back on the right track. Unfortunately, that didn't work. Once I moved in with my aunt, I began to start drinking hard liquor, doing all the things that I should not have been exposed to at fourteen. You see I came from a family that was very close-knit and loving, there wasn't anything they wouldn't do for each other but they all liked to drink liquor, Bacardi dark to be exact. They were what we would call today functional drinkers, they worked hard every day, paid their bills on time, saved money, and took care of themselves and their homes well. But I can remember my aunt always having her Budweiser beer and her pint of Bacardi dark in the kitchen cabinet. If she wasn't working, she was sitting on the front stoop or in her bedroom window with her glass of beer close and she would frequently visit that kitchen cabinet to get a drink of her stash of Bacardi. As a kid, I didn't fully grasp what this meant, but looking back, it was clear how much alcohol was a part of the everyday rhythm in her home.

I started smoking Newport cigarettes and drinking beer and liquor. She would give me money for my cigarettes and beer as needed, well actually there was nothing that she would not do for me she loved me beyond words and spoiled me like no other. My aunt being old school figured she would rather see me at home in the house drinking rather than to be out in the streets drinking. Aunt Sue was one of a kind and I do miss her great deal. In her mind at least she knew where I was and that no harm would come to me at the hands of another. At that time her logic made perfect sense to me not knowing that I was opening the door further for the enemy to have an open field day in my life. My aunt did the best she could with me but once my drinking progressed, I simply was out of control. During that time, I went to Lawrence High School, and I had no interest in learning, I didn't feel connected to any of my friends that I grew up with. My connection with them was only childhood experiences and we were all now in high school. They were doing the right thing, focused on their studies and I unfortunately was busy hanging out drinking, smoking and cutting classes. I knew a lot of the kids in Inwood because prior to me moving in with my aunt, my sister and I would go and spend the summers with her.

I began hanging out a lot smoking weed and drinking with my so-called friends. I was staying out very late past my curfew which was worrying my poor aunt to death. Now that she is no longer living, and I think back on things, I regret putting her and my mother through all of that heartache and stress of sitting up wondering if I was dead or alive. I found myself hanging with a lot of older guys, most of these guys were my friend's boyfriends and of course I wanted to fit in and follow the crowd, so I decided to date an older guy as well. From then to my present life, I have always dated older men. My husband today is older than me. I think that a part of me was in search of the void that I felt of not having that father figure in my life as a child. I was looking for love in all the wrong places, searching for the structure, nurturing and love that only a father can give. I quickly learned that just because a man is older than you, does not mean that they can provide for you the love and security of a father.

I never really experience the innocence of simply having a boyfriend my own age with the normality of going to a simple movie, out to eat, back then I can remember a boy your own age would take you to the movies and to eat at the Chinese spot walk you home and sit out on the front bench and that was a date. I can only recall going out like that twice in my life and I will cherish the memory always. My friends at the time did nothing but go to the park, drink forties of Old English and smoke weed every day of the week. I often felt like I was surrounded by people but still alone, desperately trying to fit in. Despite being outspoken,loud,and the life of the party, I was actually uncomfortable inside-it was just a facade. This wasn't the true me, I often found myself wondering, "What am I doing here"

Whenever there is a call on your life by God, you are set apart for his purpose, you will always feel uncomfortable in the crowd no matter how hard you try to fit it. I was not yet a leader, I was definitely a follower. There was an incident where a couple of my girlfriends and I were in the park smoking and we were unaware that the guys that we were smoking with laced the weed with something, we all were tripping out. I was hallucinating something terrible; everybody looked like a cartoon character, their faces were warped, I was seeing all kinds of bright lights and I felt like I was floating and could take on the world. We were all singing and climbing the fence in the park. I have no idea why we were climbing the fence but we were. my aunt came looking for me in the park because I of course was out too late past my curfew. When she called out my childhood name and street name Nay-Nay; she yanked me by my shirt and began dragging me back to her apartment, prompting me to curse and physically fight with her in the park- a reflection of my disrespectful behavior that I now deeply regret. My aunt was very upset and hurt by what had transpired and I cannot say that I blame her. She was fed up with my mess by this point, but she had so much love for me that she continued to put up with me.

There was a girl that I met at school named Tawana. We began to hang out during lunch together. She was one of the tough girls in school, she also always cut classes and we would often be at the same place where everyone cut class. She didnt have alot of friends because she had such a rough exterior but I got along with her. We would leave school on our lunch breaks because at the school we went to, we were allowed to leave during our lunch break to fast-food spots within walking distance of the school. Twana and I would never go to a fast food spot to eat for lunch, we would end up at her house or we would walk to the weed spot down on the beach and then go sit in the park, get high and hang out until it was time to go home. She was an only child and she began to treat me like a sister, she always had my back and looked out for me. She and I grew to love each other like sisters.

It finally came to a point where my aunt had enough of my behavior, and I went to live with my friend Tawana from school. Tawana lived with her mother and her mother's boyfriend. The way the apartment house was set up was that Tawana and her mother lived in an upstairs apartment and Tawana mother's boyfriend lived in the downstairs apartment. So, I went to live with Tawana, and her mother and their lifestyle was about to change me in ways I could not even imagine. I was thrust into having to fend for myself whereas when I was with my mother and my aunt, I was not faced with some of the things I was about to experience. I wanted to live with Tawana and her mother mainly because I had a greater level of freedom. I felt that I couldn't do the things that I wanted to do living with my aunt. I couldn't have a boyfriend or get phone calls from guys and if I did get a phone call from a guy I could only be on the phone for five minutes. I was always the one that had to leave the party or wherever we were hanging out because it was time to go in the house. If I didn't make it in the house on time she would be out looking for me to bring me home; which was embarrassing. Although I was about to have freedom at Tawana's house, I would soon discover that her household was even more dysfunctional than living at home or with my aunts.

Tawana's mother got legal custody of me and in the very beginning things appeared to be that of a normal household. After a few weeks Tawana's mom began to stay downstairs in her boyfriend's apartment and me and Tawana were upstairs by ourselves. It was like we lived on our own. Her mom was always downstairs, I can remember them always drinking and listening to music and partying more than not. Her mom used to always run upstairs and go in the bathroom and then go back downstairs afterwards. At the time I did not think anything of it. I simply thought that she was coming upstairs to go to the bathroom or smoke a joint by herself. All I knew is that she would always be in the bathroom for a long time.At one point I was cleaning up the bathroom in the upstairs section where Tawana and I stayed. I began to remove the toilet seat cover that every household had on their toilets back in the 80's-90's. As I began cleaning, I took the cover off to wipe the toilet top and I almost got stuck with a needle. Yes, that is right, there was a needle and syringe hidden underneath the toilet cover. I was naive to anything that pertained to drugs at that time and so I did not really put two and two together at that moment.

Tawana's mom would always have me walk with her to the projects in Far Rockaway and have me wait outside of the building while she went inside the building while she picked something up from a friend. I would be standing outside for a long time by myself, nervous and scared. I later discovered that she was not just copping, she was shooting up before she came out of the building. I always used to wonder why she had all of the undented marks on her arms and hands. This didn't seem normal to me because all of the mothers I knew had arms and hands that were scar free, soft and smooth.

My friend Tawana and I were living in the upstairs apartment fending for ourselves. We lived off of oodles and noodles and fried potatoes. This was the only thing we ate and knew how to make. We were only fifteen and didn't have money or jobs to buy food ourselves.

We finally got tired of eating oodles and noodles and fried potatoes that Tawana's uncle offered to let us help him unload things from the back of his truck whenever he would do jobs around the area. She had an uncle that used to come and pick us up to go to work with him, he would pay us for helping him load and unload things from the truck at the jobs he was doing.

After a while of Tawana and I helping him, he would then only request for me to go with him. I thought this was odd but I wanted to keep making money so that we did not have to keep eating oodles and noodles.

He had a white van that mirrored the white vans that most kidnappers would take young girls in, you know the white vans that movies portrayed as the kidnapping van.

I can remember the first time he took advantage of me in the back of that white van. He told me that if I wanted to get paid this was the way it had to be; he pushed me down pulled up my jean skirt and pulled down my panties so fast; He was trying to stick his tongue in my mouth, I wanted to vomit, he had a foul odor that turned my stomach I wanted to cry but I thought if I did it would make things worse so I held back the tears and just prayed to God that it would be over soon. I was in shock and disbelief; I was not scared but I just did nothing because I felt that there was nothing I could do, who was I going to tell and who would believe me. He told me that I better not say anything to anyone and I said nothing. My friend nor her mother ever heard of what had taken place. I did not want to cause trouble. After all he was their blood relative and I was not. I thought that if I said anything they would take his word over mine.

This was another time in my life that I did not say no! This happened every time he picked me up to go and work with him. Yes, I was sexually violated by a grown man that knew better. I just suffered in silence. After a while I would avoid going with him and would make sure that I was not around when he would come to pick me up and once he realized that I would never show up, he finally stopped coming to pick me up. Tawana and her mother never knew. Now do not get me wrong her mom was a beautiful person and like my father, she loved her daughter and myself but was caught up in the cycle of drug addiction.

Today I understand how hard life can be when you are in such a cycle. I was in no way used to this type of lifestyle, but this is what happens when you are young, searching for your identity and learning who you are. After a while, her mom was backed up on rent and went to the Department of Social Services (DSS) to get assistance in paying her back rent. They did help her by giving her money for the back rent. She asked us if we wanted her to pay the back rent or if we wanted her to give us some of the money and let the apartment go. SoTawana and I moved to Redfern projects with her grandfather. Of course, being young we said we would go live in the projects with her grandfather. Being young we were thinking that we would have some money to buy some new clothes and we would have more freedom to hang out. This was the biggest and worst decision I have ever made. Like I said I was young and knew nothing. I definitely did not know anything about living in the projects. This was a girl that grew up in Patchogue, Long Island. I was about to experience a total culture shock. My life was about to change in the worst way. The nightmare was about to begin.

When we moved with my friend's grandfather right off the back he did not like me, he did not want me to stay there. He was old and disgruntled and was a smoker and drinker. So, you never knew what you were going to get, nice or angry it depended on the day. The living conditions were not good at all. There was junk all throughout the house, dog hair and feces all over and it smelled of urine and dog. I was not used to living in such filth so I was discouraged knowing that this was now where I would be living. The room that we were to stay in was a mess. It took a lot of work for us to get it together for us to be able to sleep in. After a while he began to give me a really hard time for no reason and would lock me out every time I went out of the house.

It was to the point where Tawana had to sneak me in the house and into the room. I was not a happy camper at all, I felt trapped. It seemed to get worse because we had no money, her mom wasn't helping us in any way, shape or form, the grandfather was too busy laying in his room drinking and smoking cigarettes. Tawana and I spent a lot of time outside because it appeared that everything was good, we dressed nice, and never let anyone know what we were really going through. One thing is for sure this was no way for two young girls to live, trying to scrape up money for food and the simple daily necessities teenage girls would need.

My aunt Sue and my other two sisters lived close by in walking distance, so I was able to go over there and shower, eat and get a few bucks when I needed. Unfortunately, my aunt was ready for me to come back to live with her and she would do anything for me, so she washed my clothes and did whatever they could for me when asked. Tawana's grandfather took ill and was removed from the home, having to be put into a nursing home and was not coming back. So me and Tawana, whom I considered to be like my sister, cleaned the apartment from top to bottom and made it livable and comfortable, we both had our own room and I thought to myself finally I can have some peace and rest. It was just me and Tawana. We got along very well, we were tight, and took care of each other, she confided in me and I in her. We shared our hurts, pains and a deepest darkest secret. We made the best of things and worked with what we had.

Chapter Two

One hit and you're hooked

My friend had two cousins named Tasha and Tamika that live in the projects as well and we spent a lot of time at their house. It was there that I was introduced to the drug that destroyed my life. I can remember that it was the year of 1988 there was a new drug hitting the streets called crack cocaine (which was cocaine cooked up into a rock form) and the news was saying one hit and you are hooked. This drug was not prejudice to say the least. If you tried it, you were hooked regardless of your nationality, ethnic background, and financial status. This thing was hitting those that lived in the rich neighborhood and those that lived in the ghetto. Everyone young and old was selling this new drug for cheap and on the outside looking in it seemed like everyone was hooked. Whether they were smoking it in a pipe, smoking it in cigarettes or in a blunt cigar. One thing is for sure is that people across the United States were gripped by this epidemic and unfortunately, I was one of them.

I was fifteen at the time, living in the projects where I really didn't know anyone besides Tawana and her two older cousins. I was not yet street smart, I was naive to the way the street game went. I was used to growing up in Long Island and compared to the projects Long Island would be considered the suburbs. To my unawares Tawana's older cousin Tamika was already smoking crack and already consumed and heavily in her addiction. I had never seen anyone addicted to drugs before, so I was not able to identify her as being an addict at the time. She wasn't out in the streets, or homeless, at that time she kept herself up, dressed nice and hair together. I started spending more time with her everyday. Tamika always treated me nice, and we got along well. We used to drink beer, laugh, and listen to music, dance, and get cute on the weekends ready to see what we could get into. After some time, she began to have company come to the house on the weekends and I began to notice as I sat with her and her friends that they were not just drinking and smoking weed, they were smoking something white out of a pipe. For a while they would just do it in front of me and I was cool with that. I figured they were grown and that was their business. One night as we were sitting around the table laughing, drinking and smoking weed like we always did, someone passed me the pipe. I thought it would be no big deal because Tamika and all of her friends did it and they seemed fine. I took the pipe she told me to inhale and held it in for as long as I could, so I did. I was standing up at the time and when I exhaled the high was so intense that I fell and hit my head on the wall. I then began to get paranoid looking out of windows, I was thinking that I heard the police,I was fidgety and could not keep still. I continued to smoke, and my addiction got worse, and life got even harder.

This is exactly how the enemy works. He will lure you in making things look so innocent, fun, and exciting and oftentimes they will be all of those things in the beginning but eventually they will lead to destruction. This is exactly what it means in the Scripture in 1 Peter 5:8 “be sober and vigilant; because your adversary the devil as a roaring lion, walketh about, seeking whom he may devour.”(KJV) The enemy will oftentimes work through people to their unawares, seeking to destroy one’s life, purpose, and destiny. In my case the enemy was setting the stage for a life of destruction for me and because I was young, naive, and always looking to be loved and nurtured I was easy prey for the enemy. I was too young to know that the choices I would make early on in life would etch the path and determine the course my life would take. What I have learned over the years is that there is a consequence for every decision one makes in life, some are positive, and some are negative but there is definitely a consequence.

I began spending more and more time at Tamika’s house and it seemed that all we did was get high, sit around and wait for someone to come over and get us high for free because she could never keep any money in her pocket because as soon as she got a few dollars she would smoke it up. I was only fifteen and I didn't have any means of income, nobody was really taking care of me and I was fending for myself the best way I could. I was in survival mode, which is no way a fifteen-year-old should have to spend their youth. At that age I should have been enjoying school and friends with no worries but because of the decision I made I changed the course of my life. On the weekend and on the first of the month people would get their monthly check from DSS, SSI, or some worked and got paid on Fridays. These were the party days for us smokers. People Tamika knew and some she didn't even know; random strangers would come to her house to have a place to get high and they'd have her go and buy their drugs. The people that would come over to get high used Tamika's home because they were hiding their addictions from their families.

We would be up for days at a time just smoking, there was no time for eating or sleeping just smoking. The thing with this drug was that you kept on chasing the high, it kept you feening for the next hit and it seemed like you could never get enough. Drug dealers would pay Tamika with drugs to sit in her house and sell drugs to those that came in to get high, when people would run out of money and were feening bad enough they would perform sexual favors in exchange for drugs. I found myself in this predicament on many occasions and during that time this became my means to support my drug habit. I did not have many options at that time being so young, not old enough to work and no parental guidance to help me. So, I did what I had to do to survive.

By this time, I no longer went around my aunts because I was ashamed of what I was doing and how I looked. I was a naturally petite girl but once I was hooked on drugs, I lost a lot of weight. I was already skinny and I lost about 30 pounds. I couldn't fit any of my clothes. I didn't recognize how much weight I had lost but others around me noticed. My face was much skinnier and I lost all of my little shape. Most of my clothes I had to wear multiple pairs so that they wouldn't look so skinny. My aunts in Far Rockaway still helped me by feeding me and washing my clothes but I was too embarrassed to be around them. I could see the hurt in their eyes whenever I came around, so I stayed away as much as possible. My father was also addicted to crack during this time. The difference between him and I was he had a job. My dad worked during the week and then partied on the weekends. The day my father found out that I was smoking crack, this was a very emotional and heartbreaking moment for the both of us and I will never forget this day, it is imprinted in my heart.

It was a Friday about three or four in the morning. Tamika and I were in her room. It was a good night for me and her, we had plenty of drugs to keep us going for some time before we'd have to go out and get some more. There was a knock at the door and I heard one of the drug dealers that were in the living room talking to a man, this man was trying to but some drugs but didn't have enough money and they didn't want to sell it to the man, the man was begging them and they began to disrespect the man. I heard them cursing at him and speaking to him as if he was a worthless piece of nothing. I felt bad for the man, the more I listened I realized that I recognized his voice so I looked out of the bedroom door into the living room and to my surprise the man they were disrespecting was my father, I was angry to hear the way they were treating him. I didn't want my father to know that I to was strung out on drugs but, I was so angry and hurt by the way they were treating my dad, I busted out of the room and said to my father "stop begging them, you don't have to beg them for nothing, come with me" I said. My father came in the room with me and I proceeded to give him some crack to smoke. I did not want my father to know that I was strung out on this drug as well, but at the same time I did not want to see my father being belittled by these young drug dealers that could have been his one of his kids. The disrespect was more than I could bear in my heart. My father was surprised, and I knew that he was probably hurt at the fact that his baby girl was caught up in this whirlwind of addiction and the streets, but the fact of the matter is that when you are caught up in the whirlwind yourself there is nothing you can do to help someone else no matter how much you love and hurt for them.

So instead, my dad would look out for me, and I would look out for him the best we could when we could. I had made it very clear to my dad that he could not tell me what to do because though I loved and respected him, I felt that he had lost the right to tell me what to do because he was not there to raise me. We did not hang out together on the streets but there were times that we crossed paths while being out there and in those times we would both made sure each other was okay.

There was one night where one of the drug dealers wanted me to exchange sexual favors for drugs and since I had not been to sleep in a few days and I desperately wanted to get high I followed him into the apartment building

As I began to walk into the apartment building, my father came from out of nowhere and grabbed my arm. He told me to not go into that building but since I was on my own and felt like he did not have the right to tell me what to do, I ignored him.

I don't know where my father came from, it was like he came out of nowhere and he grabbed me and told me not to go in the building with the guy, I remember I was fussing with him because I though who are you to tell me not to go in the building, I was thinking shoot I'm grown leave me alone; I know what I'm doing. My dad got a bit aggressive about things and was adamant about me not going in the building, so I didn't go in the building and I left with him. My dad knew I wanted to get high so he took me to his house and got me high there. What I didn't know was that my father had overheard the guys in the building saying that a girl was headed to the building and when I got in there, they had plans to run a train on me. God always had someone looking out for me when I didn't even know it. In this incident it was my dad. If he wasn't there the outcome would have been different. My dad wanted so badly to protect me from the streets that he told me that if I stopped hanging out in the streets that on Fridays when he got paid from work, he would come and get me and get me high at his house. Now I know this sounds crazy, but he thought like my aunts thought when they let me drink in the house, he thought to himself at least I would know where she is at and that she is safe and not in any physical harm from anyone. I tried going to his house on Fridays for a very short time. This didn't work because both of our addictions were way too big and he could not afford to support my habit and his. I needed to go and do what I had to do to support my habit which was becoming out of control to say the least.

I found myself getting sucked into my addiction more and more, I had no money, and I had no hustle. I needed a way to make money in order to get high. With this drug there was not much generosity and if it was it was with the intention of getting something in return. In the streets that saying was true "you get nothing for nothing" so I had to figure this thing out quick, fast and, in a hurry. I didn't know what my hustle would be but I knew I had to learn the street game quickly if I was going to survive.

Over the next three years, things started getting rough for me, and my addiction put me through a lot of traumatic experiences. While walking I I met a girl and we started talking. I thought she was really nice and we walked for a while. She began to tell me about her hustle and how she was making money.

She told me to come with her to a place she called the hoe stroll and at that time I had no idea what that meant, so I went with her. The place was down on the beach in Far Rockaway, it was these really dark back streets right off the water and men would drive back there looking to pick up girls to have sex with (trick with that is what they called it in the streets back then). Simply put it was prostitution. I must have been about sixteen years old at this time. I did not want to do this but all I knew was that I desperately needed to keep feeding my addiction. I found myself getting into cars with men I did not even know, doing things I never thought I would be doing. She taught me what to do, how much to charge and this is what I did. The first few times I was scared but after a while I became numb to it all. I used to zone out, during the actual act I would place my thoughts on something beautiful in order to get through it, but mentally and emotionally it was affecting me slowly. I began to feel dirty and ashamed, emotionally in despair and I felt a dark and a heavy weight over me. I think I felt heartbroken. I just could not understand why and how my life was the way it was. I was a prisoner to the drugs, and I was definitely in bondage with no way of escape. I could not see the light at the end of the tunnel. Now from time to time I would go to Tawana's house and I would try to get myself together, sleep for a few days and eat just to go back out all over again.

I hated being in a predicament whereas I had to give up myself to men to feed my addiction. It disgusted me and was really taking a toll on me in every way. It is by the grace of God that I never contracted any diseases because the things I found myself doing were unsafe and risky to say the least. I was young and pretty and a lot of men wanted to hang out with me both young and old. Hanging with these men had become unbearable, I began to make promises that I did not fulfill. I would tell them I would do certain things with them for the drugs and once I would smoke up all the drugs I would not fulfill my side of the bargain. This was now my new hustle, getting over on men. I realized I could get high and get away with not doing anything. But like everything else in life, it doesn't always last.

On several occasions I placed myself in life threatening situations and I know that it was the Lord that was watching over me and brought me out of those situations. One time I got in the car with this man, and he drove me down on a dark road on the beach. I felt uncomfortable, but I needed to do what I had to do. Well to my surprise this man pulled out a gun and told me to get out of the car. I was petrified. I thought I was going to die that night. He threw me on the roof of the car I was shaking with fear and was begging him not to kill me, he yelled at me and told me to be quiet the tip of his cold gun was pressing against my side, I was scared to move and so I laid on the cold hood of the car I could smell the ocean and feel the ocean breeze as he raped me focused only on the sound of the waves in order to block out the physical and emotional pain I was feeling. He began to yell at me and he was saying some strange stuff. I don't know what went through his mind but he began choking me and immediately, I began to pray in my mind asking God " please don't let me die here." As soon as he was done it was like he was another person full of shame and remorse, he apologized to me, paid me and made me get back in the car and dropped me off as if nothing happened. I needed to get off of the streets and find a place that I felt safe for a while. Being out in the streets jumping in and out of cars was becoming dangerous and I was feeling emotionally broken from this ordeal.

When I finally found somewhere to temporarily stay it was at a rooming house. There was a man named Charles who lived there. He was a nasty old man that always made passes at me, he wanted to be with me but i found him disgusting and I despised him

Even as I write about this man, it bothers me and makes my skin crawl. Charles used to let people get high in his room and on this particular day he left me in the room with a random man, who would always spend a lot of money to get high. So naturally because I needed to get high, I stayed in the room with him until Charles had come back. That man wanted me to have sex with him but I didn't want to. He was disgusting and I just couldn't do it. He went ballistic and grabbed a machete and held it to my neck. He was in a rage, we began to fight , i was running around the room trying to keep away from him I began screaming for help, and the man Charles busted in the room just in the nick of time, Charles put the man out and after all that I had just went through Charles got mad at me as well because I refused to be with the man, he started beating me up and then he threw me down a flight of steps and put me out I was out in the cold beat up and with nowhere to go. I didn't understand why the Lord would allow me to experience so much suffering. I was only eighteen years old when this happened . I was beat up, but my life was spared that night. My life consisted of trying to make money for my next fix, from the time I woke up until the time I went to bed. Most days I'd find myself awake for days on end and never falling asleep.   Everything about my life had become numb. I had no idea what was going on in the world, who was president, what was the latest television show, or what recent celebrity had died in the world. The only thing I was aware of was how I was about to get my next fix. When a person is engulfed in addiction this becomes the most important thing in their life and it consumes their very being.

During my time living in Far Rockaway, I was raped multiple times and its only by the grace of God i am alive today. I can remember one time I was hanging out in this abandoned truck. We all used to hang out in this big truck drinking and getting high. There was a couch in there, some chairs, and they used to keep a water cooler in there with water to drink. I was hanging in the trailer truck, and I was exhausted. I had been up for days. I don't remember falling asleep but what I do remember is that when I woke up my shirt was wide open, and my pants were undone. I have no Idea what happened to me and with whom. Everyone was gone and I was left there in the dark. When I got up, I drank some water out of the water cooler and went on about my business as if nothing happened. I didn't have time to dwell on what had just happened to me, I had to get back to getting high. No time to waste. A few days after this incident transpired, I began to feel extremely sick, I was weak with diarrhea and the chills in the middle of a heat wave, my eyes were getting yellow, and I had no idea what was wrong with me. I was eighteen years old at the time for some reason I remember that clearly. I stayed sick for a few days until finally I could not take it any longer, so I walked myself to the emergency room. It was crowded that day in the emergency room, I was sitting in the waiting room shivering to death, they had to give me three blankets and I was still shivering. When they finally called my name and brought me to the back to check me out, they asked me if I had eaten or drank anything spoiled or contaminated, I was so out of it but after they ran some test on my I learned that I had contracted hepatitis A, now for those that do not know you get this from drinking contaminated water or food. I thought back and remembered that I had drunk water from the water cooler that was in the truck that I was hanging out in. This is a perfect example of how the addictive mind thinks, I had no idea where the water in that cooler came from, but I was drinking it with no care in the world. At that time in my life, I had no knowledge of such things, but I learned a valuable lesson after that day. The doctor let me sleep there in the emergency room overnight mainly because I was so exhausted, they couldn't wake me up, so they let me sleep over night. When I finally woke up the doctor told me to drink plenty of fluids, vitamins and rest and I would get better and so this is what I did. Now this task sounds easy to follow for most people, but for me this was no easy task because I had to find a place to sleep for a few days and get money to get fluids to drink and vitamins. I stayed with someone I knew, and they were able to get me some juice and vitamins to take while I rested. After some days had passed, I began to feel better, I had regained my strength and all of my symptoms were gone and guess what? I was back off for the races; that's right I picked up where I left off chasing my next fix.

Now when the girl Tawana's mother found out that I had stopped living in the house and was out in the street smoking crack she was angry and began looking for me. Now I know she was concerned about my wellbeing as was Tawana. She loved me but she didn't know how to help me as she could barely help herself being that she was young herself and with no real good mother figure to rely on. When Tawana's mother finally caught up with me I did not get the greeting or welcome home that one would expect to get. As soon as she saw me, she started beating me like a man in the street. I can remember her beating me so badly that I crawled under one of the benches in the project and that didn't stop her, she dragged me from out under the bench and started dragging me home. I guess in her mind she thought if she beat me bad enough that would fix things. I guess she thought that she could beat me straight. But what she didn't realize is that this was one thing that even a beat down couldn't fix. I later learned that the only thing that can truly help a person be free from addiction and that is deliverance which only God can do and thank God He for me one day. Tawana's mother dragged me back to where Tawana and I stayed in the projects. Twana was overwhelmed with joy to have me back home and I was glad to be there but still desiring to keep on getting high. I wanted to live a normal life, be happy and do all the things teenagers do. But I could not shake the urge of wanting to get high. The drug was still calling me. I stayed with Twana for a short time. I managed to gain some weight back and I began to look and feel like my normal self. We started hanging out again like normal teenagers. Tawana had a boyfriend that lived in Jamaica Queens and she and I went to see him one Friday night and I met his friend named Timothy and we began seeing each other. He was a very nice guy, treated me nicely, made me laugh and he was handsome too. I enjoyed our time together and we began seeing each other on a regular basis. Like most teenagers drank 40 ounces of old English and smoked weed and like all other teenagers he had big dreams but was too focused on hanging out. After seeing Timothy for some time I discovered that I was pregnant by this time I was nineteen years old, and I was about to have a baby. I never told him that I was pregnant, instead what I did was run. Once I found out that I was pregnant I never went back to see him. Like most addicts when trouble hits your fight or flight kicks in and you either stay or fight your way out of your situation or you run as fast as you can from it. What people fail to understand is that no matter how fast and far you run your problems go with you and oftentimes your problems get bigger and harder to fix. I chose to not deal with the fact that I was pregnant, and I ran back to drugs.

Chapter Three

Lord Help, I'm Pregnant

I was now pregnant and getting high. This was a hard and dark time for me, I had no one to confide in or to help me because I was living a life of shame. I was too ashamed to ask for help and I did not want anyone to see me the way I looked. For months I indulged with no regard to the little life that was growing inside of me. I really didn't understand the severity of my situation, I simply didn't know what to do at that point. As I think back, I can only really remember eating one time during my pregnancy. I am sure there were more times, but I can't remember them. I definitely did not have any prenatal care in the beginning of my pregnancy. My options were few at that time and so I decided to go back to Long Island where my mother lived with my sister. Sometime after my mother sent me to live with my aunt, she and my sister moved back to Patchogue from Oneonta which is upstate NY. I desperately wanted to get myself together because I wanted my baby to be alright.

Once I got to my mother's I realized that though she and my sister both welcomed me back I felt out of place, I felt that I no longer belonged, I had been gone for so long and my life was so different from when I was last with my mom and sister. So many things happened to me over the years. I had experienced so much hurt and pain being in the streets, I know today that I was suffering from trauma, physical and sexual abuse, abandonment, rejection, depression, anxiety and even grief. Yes, that's right, grief, I was grieving the loss of the person I once was. I could no longer identify myself as the person I was before I got caught up in this cycle of addiction. This person I had become was not the true me, she was a girl trying to survive a life of drugs and the streets. In my mind I had come up with all types of reasons as to why I was feeling like an outcast, why I felt out of place at my mother's house, and I even played the blame game as to why I felt the way I was feeling. One thing I have learned over the years is that the enemy will always shine a spotlight on things making them appear to be bigger than they actually are. The enemy will make things that are not true seem true. He sends a false illusion of reality in order to keep you trapped in your mind and emotions. His goal is to cause an individual to become unstable. James 1:8 says that "a double minded man is unstable in all his ways." (KJV) This had proven to be true in my life, I was unstable in all aspects of my life, my thoughts and emotions were all over the place, I didn't know if I was coming or going most of the time. I was not yet knowledgeable in regard to the Bible, power of God or spiritual warfare and so I was not able to cast down or take into captivity any of my thoughts at that time as the Scripture instructs us to do. It says in 2 Corinthians 10:5 "Casting down imaginations, and every high thing that exalteth itself against the knowledge of God and bringing into captivity every thought to the obedience of Christ"(KJV) I was in no way ready to apply that passage of Scripture to my life or any other Scripture for that matter, but the Lord would one day change that for me.

I didn't stay at my mother's house for long, a few days at best, I just didn't feel comfortable. I believe that shame had a grip on me and I felt like everyone was looking down on me, when in reality I am sure they were just hurt and concerned for my wellbeing but didn't know how to handle the fact that I was strung out on drugs. I felt so bad when I left my mom's house all types of thoughts were running through my head, I went back to Far Rockaway crying and emotionally distraught because I didn't know what to do next. I had taken a watch that belonged to my mother and while I was getting off the train on my way to the dealer to try to sell that watch, I ran into a guy they called him "Black" of course that wasn't his real name but that was his street name.

He asked me if I was going to sell the watch and I said yes, he told me not to sell the watch because I would not get much for it. Instead, he took me with him to his house and we hung out that night. By this time my stomach was beginning to show I was about four months pregnant. He asked me if I was pregnant and I responded to him honestly and told him my situation. He immediately began to talk to me about my current state of being pregnant and using drugs, this was the first person that really showed me genuine concern, he was not concerned with us getting high or having sex with me, he wasn't trying to take advantage of me in any way. I liked him and from that first day I felt a sense of peace and safety. He lived with his cousin. Her name was Tracy, she was pregnant as well. Tracy and I got along from the first day I came to their house. For the first few weeks I did nothing but eat and sleep, and was no longer using any type of drugs, he made sure of that. It was nice to feel like a family, me, Tracy and Black all trying to better our lives and looking out for one another making sure we stayed on the right track. For some time, black and I were just friends but after a short while we became a couple. I started going to the doctors to get prenatal care and was eating right and getting the rest that I needed. I was no longer using any type of drugs and I was starting to feel good about myself. Black began to help me in so many ways I must say he taught me a lot about becoming responsible. He took me to social services to help me get assistance, helped me get my I.D, get a job off the books and get my first apartment. Black taught me how to be street smart and to stand on my own two feet without having to depend on a man that would try to take advantage of me or anybody else for that matter. I didn't know how to do any of these things prior to meeting him and so in that aspect I am grateful for him coming into my life at a time that I so desperately needed. The months went by quickly and I was due to have my baby girl soon. Black and I were preparing to move into our first apartment and things were going well. My relationship with my aunts was good, I was going to visit them on a regular basis now that I was clean and they were happy for me that I found someone that was helping me get myself together. I decided to go and visit my mother one weekend. Black and I took the LIRR to my mother's house and it was our plan to stay overnight and then return back to Queens the next day but in the middle of the night I began to have some pains. My mother woke up and said to me "girl you are in labor" I thought to myself how can this be I am only seven months pregnant, well to my surprise I was in labor and about to have this baby. The ambulance came and rushed me to Brookhaven hospital. When I got there, I went right into the delivery room. My water never broke, I had what they call a dry birth so it was a bit more painful, but my labor was not long. Within an hour my beautiful baby girl was born. She weighed only 2 pounds and 11 ounces being that she was born so early. My due date was December 31st and I had her on October 13th. She was taken by helicopter to Stony Brook Hospital to go into the NICU for premature-babies. The hospital I was in did not have a maternity department. She was so tiny but so beautiful, my little angel. After about a week I had her transferred to St.

John's Hospital in Queens because traveling back and forth to Stony Brook was becoming difficult and very expensive. Once she was in the new hospital, I went to visit her every single day. Now because she was so small her respiratory system was not fully developed, she had a feeding tube, an emergency blood transfusion and she stayed in the hospital for a month until she reached four and a half pounds. The hand of God was truly in the midst of me having Shanikua early. Oftentimes we don't understand why things happen the way they do in life but God knows all things that pertain to our present and our future. Having Shanikua early saved her life and allowed her to be born drug free. If she was not born early, I cannot say with assurance that the outcome would have been the same. After a month my baby girl was to be released. Prior to her release we had to take a CPR class because the doctors explained that oftentimes premature-babies forget to breathe. She came home wearing a heart monitor. I was a young new mother trying to stay clean and care for my baby that was coming home with some challenges. Black and I moved into our own place. The apartment was small but it was my own and a place to call home.

Things went well for a short while, black got me an off the books job in Queens Bridge as a secretary. It was my first real job and I was excited. The only thing was I had to travel to work and back by myself by bus and train. This was not good for me at all. The enemy has a way of attacking your mind when you are alone. I began to start thinking about going to hang out and get high every time I traveled to and from work. The urges grew stronger and stronger as the days went on until finally one day, I found myself in the crack spot getting high, that's right I never made it to work that particular day. I thought to myself "Nay-Nay what have you done?" Just like that, in an instant my life went from good to bad, that's all it takes, one bad decision and you can find yourself on the road to destruction. Nay-Nay was my childhood nickname which followed me all the way until my sober adult years. I no longer go by that name, when God changed my life, He changed my name. But back then on the streets everybody knew me by my nickname. I never made it to work that day and never made it home either. I spent all my money and reality was beginning to sink in. I was sitting in the spot not knowing what I was going to do. The people I was there with didn't care about me or my situation, and they were only my friends while I had money to spend. Once the money was gone, they were gone. I was scared to go home because I knew I had messed up but at the same time I knew I needed to go home because my baby was home with black. Now I know I stated that black had helped me get my life together and he did. But there is a good and a bad side to everyone and his bad side was about to come out and show its ugly head. Black had grown pretty close to my Aunt Sue, Geneva and Yvonne, they liked him a lot mainly because I seemed to be doing good once we got together. He went to my aunts to seek help because I had been gone for three days and he had the baby and wanted to go and look for me. When my aunts heard that I never came home from work and that I left him with the baby for three days they were furious. They told him that when he finds me, he needs to "beat my behind" and I guess he took this literally and as a green light to start beating on me. This is why it is important that we are very careful about the words that we speak. Oftentimes we will speak words lightly, but not realizing that we are giving the enemy permission to cause havoc in our lives or the lives of others. In my case my aunts without realizing it gave him permission to beat on me. I know this was not their intent, they loved me beyond words, there wasn't anything that they wouldn't do for me but nevertheless permission in so many words was granted. As soon as he found me, he dragged me out of the spot and began to beat on me. I was getting beat down in the streets and no one dared to stop him because he was crazy, people feared him and weren't willing to risk catching the aftermath of attempting to help me. I mean after all who I was, to those that looked on and watched me get beat up I was nothing, just another young girl strung out.

Shanikua was still at my aunt's house while he looked for me. The plan was that we were supposed to come and get her once he found me but that never happened. He took me to the house, and he started to get high with me. Now not only had I relapsed but he also was in relapse mode. This was a bad situation with both of us getting high things were going downhill fast. My aunt Sue called my mother and asked her to come and get my daughter because I did not come back to get her, and it was too hard for my aunt to care for her. My mother came and got Shanikua, at first, she was not happy about having to come and get her but once she held her in her arms, she was in love.

The dark side of black was loose and I had become a victim of sexual and physical abuse. I think this was the darkest time in my life. He began to get very possessive and controlling. I could not do anything other than what he told me to do. He began taking me to the village in Manhattan and if you know anything about the village it is a place that after dark anything goes. He began making me do things with people that I would have never thought in my life that I would do. I was being used and abused and not by choice. It was like I was his property. He claimed he was teaching me how to be able to fend for myself on the streets but honestly today I know that he was manipulating me and gaining off of my suffering. If I didn't do what was demanded of me, I had a severe price to pay. By this point I was living in complete fear, fear for my life. I was only 20 years old and in an abusive relationship. And I was mentally, physically, and sexually abused and could not see my way out of this. Who could I talk to, where could I run, I had nowhere to go and I was ashamed and felt as if no one would understand what I was going through or wouldn't believe me if I told them. One thing about Black he would make sure that even in the midst of our getting high that we always dressed nice and looked good. So, me telling someone that I was being abused was useless because it did not appear that way on the outside. No one would think that I was suffering from abuse. People thought I was just getting high, but it had become so much more than that. My self-esteem was so low I started believing all of the negative things he would say to me, I had no self-worth, I was depressed, I started looking at myself as ugly and I thought there was no hope for me. I had become numb to any type of feelings; my life was like a ship without a sail just drifting deeper and deeper into a life of torment and despair. I was consumed by darkness.

A few months went by and as if things couldn't get any worse, I found out that I was pregnant again. I could not believe it, I kept it a secret from Black for as long as I could and when I began to show I mustered up enough courage to run. I was now running for my life. There was a girl that I grew up with named Shante. I ran to her house, and she let me stay with her for a while until I could figure out what I was going to do. I couldn't go out because I was in fear that Black would find me. I was so paranoid and fearful. I kept thinking he was going to get me. By the time I decided what to do in regard to the pregnancy I was five and half months pregnant I decided to get an abortion. Shante told me about a place somewhere in the city that did two-day abortions. Now I had no idea what it entailed but I was desperate, and I knew I couldn't bring another child into the world with all that I was going through. She went with me to the clinic, and I went into the exam room. They explained to me that they were placing something inside of me and once they started the procedure the first day, I had to return the next day, or I would bleed out and possibly die. I went back to Shante's house until the next day when I was due to go back. On the second day we returned, and the procedure was completed. When they were done, I cried so hard because I didn't realize how painful it would be and how it would hit me emotionally. I was in extreme pain. It felt like my insides were cut out of me. I could barely make it back to Shante's house on the train. When I reached her house and finally laid down there was a loud banging on her door. It was Black he had found me; I remember grabbing a hammer and hiding in her closet. I was scared to death; I knew I was going to die that day. Somehow or another she convinced him that I was not there, but we knew that he would be back. Desperate and fearing for my life I called my mother in a panic. I begged her to help me, and she did. My mom and my aunt Bernice immediately came to get me within hours. I could barely stand or walk; my body was weak from the procedure. When my mom and aunt came to get me they helped me to the car and drove back to my mom's house in Long Island. I made a break for it, running for my life from a man that I once believed would be a help and benefit, but who ultimately made my life worse than before I met him. Two people addicted to drugs cannot help one another, they feed off of one another and the relationship becomes toxic. A person can't help someone else when they stand in need of help themselves. In my case I had no idea that I was sleeping with the enemy. What looks good isn't always good. You can have a piece of fruit that looks good on the outside and it appears to be sweet but when you bite into it you find that it is bitter and rotten to the core.

Chapter Four

Long Island Struggles

I stayed with my mother until I recovered from my procedure but shortly after I left. As I stated earlier, I was not comfortable being there because I was no longer the girl that she raised, this person I had become felt like a stranger in the home I was raised in. I was now in a new territory and I had used my street smart to figure out where and how I could continue to get high and that is exactly what I did. I went to a town called Bellport. I only knew a few people there, some distant family and friends of the family that I grew up with. I decided to take a chance and see what I could get into. I had learned some survivor skills and now had the gift of gab so I knew that I would be able to handle myself. It seems like everywhere you went there was somebody you knew or used to know that was now smoking. I quickly connected with some people I knew through my family or that knew my parents. Once they found out that I was getting high they showed me who was who and what was what.

Things were definitely different from in the city and it took me a minute to adjust to the way people did things. I seemed to have found some favor with many people because they knew my parents back in the days and thus, they would look out for me,the drug dealers and users alike. I didn't have a place to live, most of the time I just went from house to house and slept when I could and changed when and wherever I could. I had several hustles during my time in Bellport, none that I am proud of but this is my truth. When the Lord spoke to me about writing this particular book, he told me to share my story and to be transparent because my true testimony will cause many to be delivered and his name would be glorified. I know that by sharing my experience and how the Lord delivered me will help someone else to know that they too can make it out and be free.

Even though I was on drugs I still was a pretty young lady and this worked to my advantage. A lot of the drug dealers would give me what I wanted of course but there had to be an even exchange. Nothing was for free and the sad thing about addiction of any kind is that it will cause you to do some of the unspeakable things. I found myself selling my body for money and or drugs and this had become a daily thing and it was part of my survival. Jumping in and out of cars with strange men of all nationalities was the norm. This was no way to live, not for me or for anyone for that matter. Now I know why they say that prostitution is one of the oldest professions in the world and in some places it's even legal. But the one thing that is never spoken about is the mental, emotional and physical effect indulging in such behavior can have on an individual. For me it was beginning to affect me internally, something was happening I was becoming very angry and bitter. I was disgusted with myself and saddened by the fact that I had stood to this level. I was in a low state physically and mentally. I mean I was not raised this way; but as I think about it, I started using drugs at such a young age which prevented me from having the opportunity to be groomed and nurtured into a young lady by anyone in the right way. I didn't have a sanctified, Holy Ghost filled church mother to mother me back then.

After a while my anger and bitterness got so bad that I not only was angry with myself but I began to get angry with the men that were using and abusing me for their personal gain. I was angry with the dealers that were dangling the drugs in my face in order to string me along to do what they wanted me to do. Like a dog begging for a bone. I was angry with the men that drove down from their nice little suburban homes, leaving their wife, kids behind to sneak down to the hood to pick up a street walker (that is what they called girls that were walking the street selling their bodies) to fulfill their sick fantasies. I had enough, I was like a ticking time bomb ready to go off at any given moment. The darkness and despair were consuming me. I made up my mind that I would no longer be a victim but a victor. I started to take what I wanted every given change I got. I would get into their cars and tell them I was going to do whatever it was they requested, take their money then quickly jump out of their car. This was what I thought was my new hustle . It was my way of not having to give of myself to a man and this worked for a time until things began to get dangerous. Many of the young ladies were getting beat up and raped, some were even going missing. Most of the girls on the street were close to each other in regards to doing their best to look out for each other. We would let each other know who was safe to get into a car with and who was not. The word on the street was that it was a specific cop car that was taking girls and hurting them. We all were fearful but yet we still had to get out there and do what we had to do to survive. One of my close friends was found killed and the word on the street was that it was a certain police officer that drove car 509. I do not know for a fact if she was killed by this officer but they found her body mangled and severely beaten. The word on the street was that this was how she was killed. I was overcome with sadness, this was the first person I knew that was killed and in such a horrific way. It took me a very long time to get over her death. Her death for some reason haunted me for a long time. There was another lady I knew named Jackie, an older lady that was dear to me. She knew my father and because of that we became very close, looking out for one another making sure we both had what we needed. Late one night I ran into her, she was frantic, screaming and yelling, it appeared that she had been beat up. She told me that she had been picked up by the same police officer and that he beat her up, made her perform sexual favors and then let her go. She warned me to watch out for myself because not only did we have to watch out for the men we were jumping in and out of cars with but now we had to watch out for the police.

It was around that same time I found myself in a life-or-death situation. There was a man I used to hang out with quite often, we used to get high together and so I was comfortable being around him and I did not see him as a threat. This particular evening we were hanging out and he was acting very strange and paranoid. For some odd reason he kept on insisting that we go for a drive, so I gave in and we hopped into the car. He started to drive down this dark road, glancing around suspiciously, while I kept urging him to turn back. As we were driving something strange happened. We were approaching a stop sign and it was like the Lord was speaking to me, urging me to get out of there that danger was ahead. The stop sign was as if it was jumping out at me, saying "stop danger, danger." It was like the sign was pulsating, warning me that I was in trouble. I quickly realized that if I continued to go down this road with this man I would not make it back alive. I started yelling for him to let me out of the car, he ignored me and started driving faster. I grabbed the steering wheel and tried to get him to stop the car but he got infuriated and punched me in the face and pulled out a knife. We started to tussle and the car was weaving all over the road. I was in a panic and I opened the car door and jumped out of the moving car and ran into the woods. I was running and didn't even know where I was running to. I kept on running until I came out on the other side of the woods to a road. Once I got on the road I kept on walking until I finally reached the main road and was able to get a ride from this lady that was kind enough to stop and take me back to safety.

That was the final straw for me. After that night I decided that it was best to stop getting into cars with men that I knew and didn't know. Although my life was in shambles, I did not want to die, I was grateful to God for his hand of protection that was on me that night. Some people say that the Lord does not speak to those that aren't saved but I know without a shadow of a doubt that the Lord had angels dispatched that night. I stayed out of the car but not out of trouble. I went to one of my mother and fathers friends who was a big time drug dealer at that time and asked him to look out for me with some product and he did. It wasn't a lot but it was enough for me to change my hustle. I started selling drugs mainly to individuals coming from out of town. I thought to myself, this would keep me from jumping in and out of cars. One of the problems with a person that uses drugs is, they end up using more than they are selling which keeps them in a cycle of constantly trying to have enough to use and to buy more to sell in order to keep using. For me it was not about making big time money, it was simply about being able to support my habit and have the basic necessities I needed. I did this for some time and it seemed to be keeping me afloat but there were times I had to revert back to my other hustle. I had become very paranoid; I was paranoid about everything. Every white person I sold drugs to I thought was the police. I thought everyone was out to get me which caused me to look over my shoulder all the time. Simply put I was a mess mentally. My paranoia finally became a reality.

I was out one Friday night, and there was a lot of traffic that night. People were coming to buy drugs left and right. I was not being very couscous. I had let my guard down and was just selling to everybody, I didn't care if they looked like cops or not. I was trying to make as much money as I could. The more I made, the more I wanted. The Scripture says in 1 Timothy 6:10 "For the love of money is the root of all evil: which while some coveted after, they have erred from the faith, and pierced themselves through with many sorrows."(KJV) I was chasing the money so frantically thinking that I was on top, you couldn't tell me anything. Little did I know I was falling into the trap of the enemy, I was about to have sorrow in my life for many days.

Chapter Five

Off to Jail

A few days later I was walking down the street early in the morning to the store to buy a pack of cigarettes and the police stopped me and arrested me. I was crying like crazy and at that time I did not know the reason for my arrest. They took me to the fifth precinct and began to process me and it was during that time that I found out I was being arrested for a drug sale to an undercover cop. I stayed in the precinct overnight and on the next morning I was out on a bus to the Central Islip County courthouse. I sat down stairs in the bullpen for hours, I was so exhausted that I slept until they called my name to go in front of the judge. I was hoping to be released on my own recognizances but the district attorney was not trying to hear that, my bail was set at ten thousand dollars and I most definitely didn't have anywhere near that type of money. Since I did not have that type of money, I was off to Riverhead County Jail. When I was out on the streets it never seemed to cross my mind that I could possibly go to jail. I watched so many of my so-called friends get arrested but I never thought that I would find myself in that predicament.

I was given my green uniform, a cup and toothbrush and was escorted down to what they called the pods. As soon as I entered the pods it was like a family reunion. There were so many girls from the streets that were there. When you stop seeing certain people on the street, they are either in jail, rehab or dead. In this case many of the girls that I no longer saw on the streets were in jail. For the first week or two I did nothing but sleep and eat peanut butter and jelly sandwiches. I needed to regain my strength from all of that ripping and running I had been doing. When I finally snapped out of my daze, it hit me that I was in jail, with no idea when I'd be getting out. Since I was in my jail for selling drugs, I was moved to Riverhead County Court because it was deemed a felony. This was not looking good for me. I went back and forth to court; the lawyer that was appointed to me seemed to be genuinely concerned and was fighting for me. After some time of going back and forth to court I was finally sentenced to six months and five years' probation. I was so anxious to get out of jail that I accepted the plea not realizing then that for a person with an active addiction taking any kind of probation was a set up to go back to jail. During the next few months, I began to go to NA and AA meetings plus church services. I was beginning to feel that I had a chance at living a sober life. I began reading my Bible and saying my prayer in the morning and in the evening. I did this ritually. I was feeling good about myself and enjoyed my quiet time in my cell reading the Bible. One night I was reading the Bible in my room and I turned to the back of the Bible and there was a prayer, it was the sinner's prayer, now I had heard about Salvation and accepting Christ as your Lord and Savior because I grew up Catholic and went to religion school. That night something was urging me to get down on my knees and accept Christ as my Savior. I didn't know really what the ins and outs of being saved were but I was so compelled to make Christ my personal Lord and Savior. I got on my knees and began to recite the sinner's prayer that was in the back of the Bible. I did not understand much about Salvation if there was something particular that I needed to be doing next but I continued to read my Bible and pray daily. I felt a closeness to God and even though I was locked up I had a sense of peace. One evening while taking a shower, I noticed a lump in my breast. At first, I wasn't too concerned, unaware of the potential seriousness of such a discovery. It wasn't until one of the ladies urged me to get it checked out, warning it could be something serious, that I began to worry. Once I went to get it checked out from an outside doctor, what I discovered on my breast became serious enough for them to take a sonogram to check the size of the lump and the final decision was that I needed to get the lump removed. I returned to the dorm, went straight to my room, and began praying. I didn't ask the Lord for healing, as I didn't know I could ask for that at the time, but I prayed nonetheless. I was nervous and simply prayed.

A few days later I went back to the doctors and they wanted to do another sonogram before going forward with the removal. I first went to the nurse in the jail's medical department. We both examined the area and felt the lump. It was even visible.

After seeing the jail's nurse, I waited for transport to pick me up to take me to the outside doctor. I hated going to the doctors outside of the jail because they had to shackle you hand and foot. I was always embarrassed having to walk into the doctor's office in shackles. I already felt shameful being in jail but to have people looking at you with a look of fear and disgust is a feeling I did not look forward to feeling.

As the sonogram was being done, I saw the technician's face look strange. She kept on taking pictures, it was taking much longer than it did the first time I had the sonogram done. I began to instantly get worried. I was thinking to myself "oh God what does she see," I didn't know what to expect when she was done, I got dressed and waited in the room for the doctor to come in and speak to me in regards to when I would be getting the lump removed. To my surprise when the doctor came in the exam room, he told me that he doesn't know what happened but they did no see any lump, he examined me again feeling around in disbelief and I myself was in disbelief because I knew for as surety that just a few days ago it was there. He told me that we would not be doing any surgery because the lump was no longer there, he didn't have an answer for me as to what happened he just said that it was gone.

I got back to the jail and the nurse there could not believe that it was gone either. Days prior we both felt the lump and for it to just be gone in just a few days was sure of a miracle. It wasn't until many years later that the Lord spoke to me and let me know that he had healed me. I had prayed innocently and the Lord answered my prayer without me even realizing it.

Eventually I was released, I was leaving with the mind to do right, I had five years' probation and I thought I was ready to get myself together. I didn't stand a chance on probation. I went back to getting high and the cycle of my addiction began all over again. I believe that each time a person gets clean and then relapses their addiction gets worse and things on the street get worse for them. This is how it was for me at least. I believed that I had gotten more street smart so I began to get more reckless. I was still trying to sell drugs to people and of course in one of my acts of desperation I sold to an undercover cop again. This time, I was convicted of two drug sales and an attempted sale, landing me back in jail. My life was going downhill and by this point I could not see any light at the end of the tunnel for myself. This was it I was just going to be out in the streets, in and out of jail for the rest of my life. I was sentenced to eight months and this time I was not afraid to be in jail. I knew a lot of people there and I ran with the popular crowd. I had gone back to the pods for a short time and I began getting into fights so they moved me from the pods which was supposed to be the privileged area for the less violent or troublesome ladies. I was moved upstairs to the area where the cells were. All of the ladies who didn't know how to act, or got into many fights were sent upstairs. There were only about fourteen ladies on each section upstairs and we all had a cell. I felt more at peace up there and I stayed there for the duration of my sentence. During my time in jail my aunts took care of me. They would buy me the clothes I needed and would send me money weekly and I appreciated that because I didn't have anyone. There was only one time where my mom came to visit me in jail but shortly after she stopped. She couldn't handle seeing her daughter sitting in jail, wearing green clothes and inside of the jail walls. I understood why she only visited once. I didn't care about receiving visits; they only served as a reminder that I couldn't go home afterward.

After being released from jail, I went to stay with one of my older cousins until I could find a place of my own and find a job. By this time I was doing really well. I wasn't getting high and I was focused on getting my life back on track to become the young woman that I knew that I could be. I was trying my best to get my life together because I wanted my daughter Shanikua to live with me. So I got a job working at 7-eleven and shortly after that I found a place to live. I was living in a rooming house within walking distance from where I worked. I had a big furnished room, a refrigerator and a hot plate so I was able to cook if I desired. I was happy. It made me feel good about myself that I was able to go to work every day and support myself with a new and legal hustle. I would see my mom and my daughter a lot. Things were beginning to work out for me but the enemy is always lurking. The enemy was just waiting for an opportunity to drag me back into the streets.

There was a very nice guy that also lived in the rooming house, he invited me to his room one night. I was lonely and didn't have any friends since no longer doing drugs. All of my friends were drug addicts and I didn't want to surround myself with them.

Not thinking anything of hanging out with him, I went over to his room to hang out. When I entered his room, he had a crack pipe sitting on the table. I tried to ignore it but the temptation was too much for me and before I knew it, we were getting high. I went back to my room feeling bad about having relapsed. I thought to myself "what have you done?" I continued to go to work trying to get back on track but I was still getting high whenever I hung out with my neighbor. After a while that wasn't enough for me my urges were getting stronger, I needed to find my own connection and because of what I previously learned about the streets I did.

There were a few guys that would stop in all the time and I would let them steal beer and I'd give them free packs of cigarettes. One of the guys was named Jerome, yes Jerome my husband. The Lord would many years later bring us together. One night I asked my cousin's husband where I could buy some drugs and he at first was shocked and upset to hear that I had relapsed but eventually he took me to someone's house. We called them the little people because they were both midgets. I started going there to get high and every time I went there Jerome would be there as well, we became friends and would get high together. I was at that time trying to get high but keep my life in order by working and keeping my place. It was becoming very hard for me. I eventually lost my job because I would stay out all night and then be too high to go to work. Once I lost my job, I had no stability at all and I eventually lost my place to stay. I was out on the street with nowhere to go once again. I ran into Jerome out on the street one night and he took me to where he stayed. He stayed in a room as well and he let me crash there for a good while. We were both getting high, trying to find ways to make more money so that we could continue to get high.

Jerome was always nice to me, he never had a secret agenda, I liked him a lot. I was always able to be myself around him and I considered him a friend. He was the only one I could talk to about my true feelings, hurts, pain. I could be vulnerable around him and he would not use it to his advantage. We looked out for each other. There was another girl Jerome used to let stay there too, her name was Dotty. Each of us had our hustle and we all looked out for each other the best we could when we could. Even though Jerome and I were in the friend zone we were intimate with each other on many occasions when we hung out. We both would get paranoid when we would get high together but Jerome would be bugging out. People hated getting high with him. I mean they hated getting high with me too but for some reason when we got high together, I could calm him down, he was comfortable with me and I was comfortable with him. I loved Jerome because I felt that he genuinely cared about me regardless of drugs or money. Seems like the months turned into years, I went back and forth from Patchogue to Bellport getting high, house to house, in and out of cars. This was my daily ritual, nothing else seemed to exist or seemed to matter. I was losing so much weight I didn't even recognize this person I had become. Me and Jerome always ran into each other while out there and when we did, we would hang out. I always had to be on the move, always trying to make the next dollar. To be honest I can't even say that I gave myself a chance to even enjoy the high because I was so busy trying to make sure that I never was without. It was not a good feeling to be desperate for the next hit and not have any money to get it. In those times things got really ugly and I hated to be in that position. I had lost so much weight that I had to wear two pairs of pants. I even walked for so long I walked the heels completely off of my shoes. By this time in my life, I had done a lot of things that I am not happy about, I had been with a lot of people all for the wrong reasons and I still seem to be chasing a high that I could not obtain. I was in a vicious cycle. Lord, when would this end for me.

As if things could not get any worse, I was pregnant again. Not that I didn't desire to have another child but

I didn't want any more children in the predicament that I was in. I knew that this wasn't the type of lifestyle conducive to raise any children. I couldn't even raise my daughter so why would I want to bring another child into the world. I was still getting high trying to figure out what I was going to do, I knew I had to stop using but it wasn't that easy because for one I didn't have a place to stay where no one was using.

One cold winter night a man picked me up and he noticed that I was pregnant. I instantly started to cry, I had sold my coat for drugs. I was freezing, alone and dying to get high. His name was Kevin, he was a decent man. He took me to his house that night. I was so glad to have a nice hot shower, I could wash my hair, eat a real good meal and sleep in a nice warm house. I slept for days and upon waking up he told me that I could stay there but I could no longer get high or have anyone in the house. He trusted me to stay at his house when we would go to work, I was extremely grateful. Now don't get me wrong he wanted things in exchange and this part of it I didn't like but it was better than being out on the street. So, I made the best of it. Eventually I got bored with being in the house by myself with no one to talk to. I started having people that I knew would buy me drugs and bring it to the house before Kevin came home from work. I even saw Jerome a few times and he would go and get drugs for me. He was the only one I would let in the house. After a month or so I left Kevin's house because I was rested and tired of playing house. It was starting to mentally bother me. I could no longer bear being in a sober state of mind and doing activities with Kevin that made my skin crawl. I wanted out, so I left and went back to being on the streets.

What I have learned is that a lot of times men and women continue getting high because they can not deal with the reality you feel when you are sober. Being sober only meant you had time to think about what you are doing and what your life has become. I got high because I was addicted but I kept on getting high because I needed to numb the pain and reality of what I had been suffering on a day-to-day basis.

I got locked up again and this time I was thanking God, I was glad to be going to jail. I was able to get off the cold winter streets and my baby would be drug free. I was about four months pregnant when I got locked up. I started to gain weight, the baby was kicking and I was happy being able to experience all the things a mother experiences during a normal pregnancy. I was getting the proper prenatal care and doctor visits from an outside doctor. As I stated earlier on, I hated the fact of being handcuffed and shackled every time I had to go to the doctors. I was even more ashamed of being pregnant. After a while I learned to get over that feeling and figured that as long as I was getting what I needed for my baby, no one else's opinions of me mattered. I was overjoyed when I had my sonogram and found out that I was having a boy. My days were full of laughs and happiness as long as I focused on the joy of being pregnant. But in the midnight hours I wondered what was going to become of me and the baby.

They were trying to send me to an upstate Jail to do my time. The first offer they gave my lawyer was two to four years. They told me that I could bring my baby with me and that I would be in Bedford Hill Correctional facility. The idea of having my baby with me was great. But I didn't want to raise a baby in prison. I didn't even want to go to prison for that matter. Bedford Hills is not like a county jail, its prison. It is a maximum prison, the ladies that are there are doing hard time for major crimes. I would have to go and stay at Bedford Hills if I wanted to keep my baby with me. Bedford was the only prison that allowed you to have your child with you if the child was born while you were in prison and they were able to stay with you for up to twenty-four months. My lawyer continued to fight for a better deal and he got one. He requested that I go to a long-term in-patient drug program. At that point I was willing to do anything to prevent me from having to go upstate. I would be able to keep my baby and go to the program. The program was called Apple and they had a mother daughter house that was in Ronkonkoma. I was praying that all would go as planned and that I would be accepted into the program. I waited patiently as I went back and forth to court for a final answer.

I spent most of my days playing spades with the ladies, this passed the time and made jail time go faster. It wasn't good to be in your head all of the time worrying about what was going to happen to you. A person would drive themselves crazy doing that. I learned to pass the time by playing spades and reading books. I read a lot of books including the Bible. It helped me to pass the time. I was playing cards one day with some of the ladies and I said to them that I thought I had a urinary tract infection because I kept slightly urinating. They started laughing at me and said "girl your water broke you about to have that baby" I thought to myself they are crazy I didn't even feel any pain. Shortly after that I went into full blown labor. It was time, my baby boy was coming. I was nervous and scared at the same time. All of the girls were yelling with joy, they were not going to see me again because once I had the baby I would be moved to the maternity ward. I was sent down to the medical department and waited for transport to take me to the Riverhead hospital and yes even in labor they shackled you during the transport. Thank God, they didn't shackle me during the delivery. After a few pushes my baby boy was born 7 pounds and 11 ounces. He was beautiful, he had a head full of hair and was healthy and strong, simply perfect. I was in love instantaneously. I decided to name him Maliek, I named him after the guy that played in the television show New York undercover, the name Maliek means king and he was my little king. I stayed in the hospital for two days, each day they would bring Maliek to my room so that I could bond with him but every night like clock work they would take him back to the nursery. They had a guard outside of my door twenty-four hours a day and my foot stayed shackled to the bed. I couldn't wait to get out of there and go back to the jail. The jail maternity was inside of the medical department. It was a large room and it held up to four inmates and their babies. When I got to the maternity ward there were already two other girls there. One girl was about to be released and the other girl named Pam was also waiting to go to the Apple inpatient program. She also had a little boy. Her son's name was Patrick and he was a few days older than Maliek. After the other girl went home it was just Pam and I with our boys. We got very close while we were there. After about two weeks Pam left to go to the program. I was happy for her but I was also sad because I was left there alone. Even though I had Maliek with me there was no one else to talk to, or play cards with or to help me if I needed help with Maliek. I was a new mother, I didn't have any mothering skills, not for a newborn baby. I stayed in the maternity ward for about two more weeks. By this time, I was getting used to being alone, just me and Maliek and was enjoying the bond that I had with him. I was feeling joy down on the inside because of the beauty of my beautiful baby boy. He gave me a sense of hope.

Chapter Six

Rehab or Relapse

My day was finally coming. I was sentenced to the program but if I did not complete it, I would be sent back to jail. A few days after my sentencing I was off to the program. I was nervous because I had heard that the program was tuff and had a lot of rules but I had no choice but to make the best of it for me and Maliek. There were three big houses on the property: the woman's house, men's house and the mother and child house. Of course, I was in the mother and child house, the first person I saw there was the girl Pam I had been with in the maternity ward in jail. I was glad to see a familiar face and I was glad I had Maliek with me, it made things a little easier. Being there definitely was different and took a lot of getting used to. We were made to get up bright and early to get our children dressed and fed and taken down to the nursery for the day while we cleaned and studied the program steps. The steps we had to memorize were to transform our way of thinking. It was teaching us things like honesty, trustworthiness, respect and so on. The thing I remember the most is that the days were long and hard filled with a lot of work and after a day of work we had to care for our children. I eventually got the hang of it all and found myself excelling. I even started going to school there for my G.E.D. The girls would watch Maliek for me in the evening on certain days so that I could walk over to the woman's house for class. One of our work assignments was to work in the nursery with the kids. I loved doing that assignment because I would get to see Maliek during the day and it was better than buffing and waxing the floors, washing baseboards or cutting the grass in the heat. I adjusted well to being there, I followed the rules and applied myself. I was feeling good about myself and my small accomplishments, I passed my G.E.D test and got my driver's license and before you know it, I was in the final stages of the program. The final stage of the program was called Re-Entry. This was where they sent you out to find a job. You were done with the program and were preparing yourself to go back into society, once you found a job you would work on buying a car, and saving to rent an apartment for yourself and baby. I found a job on the first day I went out to look for one. I got a job at an assisted living facility around the corner from the program. I was doing really well, saving a lot of money and learning how to be responsible in hopes to live a productive life. I came home from work one evening to find all of the ladies sitting in chairs. They were all in the guilt seat is what they called it. This was where everybody had to tell what they knew about each other, in other words snitching on each other. Nobody there was getting high or anything like that, well not to my knowledge but we all did things we weren't supposed to when we went on home visits or when we chaperoned one of the other ladies on their home visit. I mean some of the girls would meet up with their boyfriend instead of going to their approved visit place, some had cell phones or money when they weren't supposed to and they wanted to know who was doing what. When I got there one of the girls was crying because they were being penalized for whatever was told that she did, she had lost her privilege to go home. When I saw that I refused to sit in the guilt seat with the rest of the ladies. I had come too far in the program and was on my way out the door. I was no longer mandated there; I was still there only because I was still getting myself together. I couldn't bring myself to spill all the dirt on the ladies. I knew a lot of stuff about the ladies because at that point I had been there a long time and I just couldn't do it. So, I packed up my stuff and left. I put Maliek in the stroller and walked back to my job, picked up my check and left. I called for a ride from a friend that worked at the program and they picked me up and took me to a hotel that was in Patchogue. I had money so Maliek and I were able to stay in the hotel for a few weeks until I found a permanent place to stay and find a cheap car. One of my friend took me into town to the laundromat to wash cloths, I stepped outside of the laundromat to smoke a cigarette and while I was outside, I looked down the street and saw a man walking and I said to myself "I know that walk" I couldn't believe my eyes, I started to get excited and I called out to him. It was Jerome. He turned around and when he saw me, he had a big smile on his face. I ran to him and gave him a big hug. I was so happy to see him. It was my friend, my confidant, my ride or die. Jerome looked so good he had gotten himself clean, gained all his weight back and was thriving. He was on his way to work that day and so I didn't hold him up but we exchanged numbers and stayed in contact. I was looking for an apartment and so when I reached out to Jerome, I asked him if he knew of anything and I was glad when he expressed to me that one of his co-workers was renting an apartment. He took me to look at the apartment and I decided to take the apartment. It was a one-bedroom apartment in Mastic Shirley. Things were working out. I had my own place and still had my job and brought a cheap car to get around in, I was grateful and glad to have my own. I started going to NA meetings with Jerome. This was helping me to stay connected and stay on the right track. Jerome was showing me such love and support as he always did, even when we were out on the streets getting high together, he always showed me love and respect. He would do anything in his power to help me. Jerome was going to church and making his meetings, he was focused and there was a glow about him. He was talking about the Lord and in the meetings expressing what the Lord was doing in his life. I was amazed at how the Lord was changing his life and how different he had become.

After some time, I started seeing a guy from my past which I thought I loved but I didn't even know what the meaning of love was. I started using drugs at such a young age that I never had the opportunity to experience real love. All I knew revolved around drugs, hurt and pain. I should have known that once you come out from a negative lifestyle you are not to go back to entertain anything or anyone. Unfortunately, I followed my heart and not my mind and got into this relationship that caused me to relapse again. I was looking for love in all the wrong places and it was leading me to destruction every time and this time was no different. I got into this relationship, and it led me to a major relapse, this relapse caused me many great losses. I lost my apartment. Eventually, I did find another apartment in Strathmore Ridge, but things were going downhill very quickly. I did not know how long I would be able to keep my head above water. I was no longer in contact with Jerome because I knew he was doing the right thing with his life, and I did not want to get him involved with my drama. When I moved to Strathmore Ridge, I moved in with this guy and I eventually lost my job and was months behind in the rent. I stopped seeing this individual because he went to jail and by this time, I was all messed up by then. My mom lived a few doors away from me with my daughter Shanikua who was probably around ten years old by this time. I knew that my mother knew something was wrong based on my behavior so I avoided her as much as possible. There was a drug dealer that hung in the complex and of course he made himself known to me. He started coming to my house at night to sell drugs. I knew that this was a bad idea but he was feeding me drugs. Since it was hard for me to go out with a baby, I allowed him to come over. This only lasted for a month or so because I eventually lost the apartment. I was so disappointed in myself and suffering from depression and despair, I felt like giving up but Maliek was my only ray of light, he was the only thing that helped me hold it together as much as I could until the day came that I couldn't hold it together any longer. Now this drug dealer had a friend with him and one night I slept with this guy. I honestly couldn't even tell you his name; I probably didn't even care I slept with him for drugs one night in a desperate state of mind. Well, I learned a valuable lesson and that is to never just react quickly when doing something, I learned to think things through before I do them because through that one quick meaningless encounter, I got pregnant again.

Eventually I got out of my apartment and Maliek went to stay with my mother because I just couldn't handle trying to get high and have my son with me. There were times I would leave him with people that I considered friends but wouldn't come back for days. I knew this was not cool and I thank God for my mother because she stepped in and took my son in a time that I so desperately needed. She always told me not to worry about the kids and to just take care of myself. She always let me see my kids and never spoke bad about me to them. I didn't see them that much because I would only go around them when I was looking decent and had money to bring them something or had time to spend with them. I didn't go around them when I was high and so I stayed away most of the time. I went to Bellport and started getting high again this time I was getting high with a vengeance. I didn't care about anything, not myself and definitely not this baby I was carrying.

I was out there, homeless and living for the next opportunity to get high. I would go from one house to the next getting high and when I wasn't doing that, I was trying to make money to continue getting high. It was a crazy cycle and my mind wasn't even on the fact that I was still pregnant. I just didn't care anymore. I had accepted the fact that this was it for me, that there was no way out of this bondage I was in. I was more than likely going to die in the streets.

Months had gone by and I was still running around, looking and feeling terrible and the poor child I was carrying was involuntarily along for the ride. One night I was at this ladies' house and I went into labor. I went to the hospital with my drugs and my crack pipe in my pocket, I didn't even want to go but once those labor pains hit you there's no turning back, this baby was coming whether I wanted it to or not. When I got to the emergency room I was crying because I knew that this was not going to turn out good. By this point I was sobering up and reality was hitting me in the face. The doctor was treating me very coldly. I could feel his anger and disgust, he was looking at me as if to say " here goes another crackhead delivering a baby on drugs." This may have been the case, but I was more than just a woman on drugs having a drug addicted baby, I was caught in a vicious cycle, I didn't want to have this child strung out on drugs, and I didn't want to be on drugs. I wanted what every other woman wanted in life and that was to be happy, sober, married, in love and all of the other good things that come in life.

Unfortunately, that wasn't the case and it hurt me that I was being judged at that moment. In a few pushes the baby was born, It was a boy. I named him Kalief; he weighed only four pounds and they took him from me right then and there, they called Child Protective Service. I never saw him again.Deep down inside I felt like I was a bad mother because I had put this drug over the care and well-being of my unborn child. My addiction was more important than my child. This made me do drugs even more. I could not deal with the feelings of sadness and despair that I felt when sober. Now this is how the mind of an addict works. I immediately got up after delivering the baby and walked out and went back to getting high with no regard. When I think about it today I can't even fathom doing something so crazy but that's exactly what I did at that moment. I didnt think about what I did and I didn't talk about it after. I just moved on, I blocked it out of my memory, I pushed those feelings way down, they were simply too hard to deal with. The only thing I knew to do was to keep on using so that I could numb the feelings of my harsh reality and that is what I continued to do.

After a while I got tired of the old way of making money and I needed more money in larger amounts, my addiction was increasing and I needed to do more and at a faster pace, so I started to boost or in layman's terms I started stealing. I linked up with this guy named Skip. He was my driver and lookout. Every morning we would make a game plan of which stores we would go to and who we were going to sell the merchandise to. We had our customers that would give us orders, some were dealers and others were just people in the neighborhood. Everybody was looking for a deal; they didn't care if it was stolen or not. We did this for a very long time together. We were not in a relationship; we were just business partners and we worked very well together. I was seeing someone else I had met on the street. His name was Sydney and I eventually started staying with him at his sister's house. My problem was that I always had to be out running around in those streets. I could really never sit still and so the only time I was really ever in the house with Sydney was when I was planning to sleep, eat and change clothes. After a few days I would be off for the races again. He was a nice guy but I wasn't in any way ready for any type of commitment and neither was he. I don't think we really knew how we were both blinded by addiction. Nevertheless he was kind to me and so was his family, they were there for me even though they had their struggles as well.

Eventually my luck began to run out and the boosting business was drying up. I began to get fearful probably because I was pregnant again. That's right I was pregnant again this time with Sydney's baby. At least I knew who the father was, not that it made my circumstance any better.

One day I went into the store Kmart to steal some baby clothes for someone. I was beginning to show I was probably about four to five months pregnant and as I was leaving the store an undercover security stopped me. We were tussling back and forth, I was trying to get away from him and to no avail he picked me up and slammed me on the concrete. This guy was really taking his job to the extreme, as if he were the police. My lookout jumped out of the car and helped me and I was able to jump in the car and get away. That was the last time I went into anyone's store. My boosting days were over.

That same night skip and I went to some ladies' house that he knew. She lived in a rich neighborhood. It must have been two or three in the morning. Skip went to bring her some product. When we got there, he saw that she had a stack of money hanging out of her pocketbook and he told me to take it. The plan was that he was going to distract her in the other room while I took the money and at the time the plan sounded very simple, I would take the money and we would leave without her noticing. Well things don't always go as planned. I took the money and Skip and I were trying to leave quickly and as we went to sneak out the ladies sliding glass patio doors I slipped and fell. It was early morning and there was frost on the ground. The lady heard us sneaking out of the door and she started chasing us so we jumped in the car and locked the doors. She looked frantic, screaming and banging on the car windows. Skip tried to back the car out of the driveway so that we could make escape. The lady desperately wanted to catch us, so she jumped on the hood of the car, while he was still backing up. Her body began swinging back and forth on the hood of the car. This was pure insanity, not only on her part but on ours as well. This was like something straight out of a movie. I was yelling to stop the car but he wouldn't, the lady had a look in her eyes that I will never forget; she was like a raging lunatic. She flung off the car and landed in the front yard in the grass and we took off. As I looked back, I saw her standing in the street yelling and screaming at the car as we drove away. We had got away; but no good thing comes from doing other people wrong and this I would soon find out. We made off with quite a bit of money and of course the first thing we did was buy a lot of drugs to last us for a little while. We thought what we bought would be enough to last but we were wrong.

We checked into a hotel room that would not be well known by the police and got a nice hot meal, showered and relaxed after our crazy money heist. We were exhausted, high and paranoid because of what we had done. Hours passed by and there was a knock at the door. Skip looked out the hotel door peephole and it was the police. We panicked, hid the drugs and Skip thought it was a good idea to open the door for them.

Still to this day I do not know what was going through his mind. When we opened the door they told us that they had us on camera stealing out of a drug store. They had no idea what we had done earlier that night but were there because we were suspected in an incident at a drugstore and they wanted to question us. They couldn't arrest us then because they didn't have a search warrant but they did let us know that they were on to us. This was bad. We didn't know what to do after they left, we waited until it was time to check out and we left and a few hours later they picked us up and arrested us. I never really understood why they didn't arrest us at the hotel that night but once we left, they picked us up. Once we got to the precinct, they first separated us and began to question us, trying to play one against another so that we would snitch on each other. There was another lady also locked up at the table next to me and I knew her we hung out together. It was only a week or so prior that we were all boosting together. Once I saw her there, I knew that we were all there for the same thing and that it was from the innocent that transpired at the drugstore that she had stolen from. Skip had driven to the store to boost cartons of cigarettes. I didn't want to go boosting that day because I was exhausted. Now let me remind you that I was still pregnant while all of this was going on. Skip drove her and I rode with them. I sat in the front seat of the car while she went into the store to do what she had to do. We were parked right in front of the door. All she had to do was move quickly and get the cigarettes and run and jump in the car. She got the cigarettes and jumped in the car but one of the lady workers ran out behind her trying to be the hero. She got so close to the car, we ended up running over her foot. We were all not going home, we stayed in the precinct that night and rode the bus to court that morning. Now we all thought that we would get a small bail or a twenty-to-thirty-day sentence and be back on the streets in no time but boy did we have a rude awakening. When each of us went in front of the judge, bail was denied and the District Attorney said that the case was to be moved to County Court in Riverhead which was a felony court. We couldn't understand this because she only stole two cartons of cigarettes and anything under a thousand dollars' worth of merchandise was considered petty larceny. I was appointed an ATB lawyer and when I met with him, he explained to me that during the drug store incident being that the lady's foot got run over it was no longer considered a misdemeanor but a felony and not only a felony but a violent crime. This was not looking good for me because I already had two past felonies under my belt. To top it all off we were connected in this case as co-defendants. The first offer that was given to us was four to eight years, which none of us accepted. They were trying to get each of us to testify against each other in order to get a lesser plea deal but we were not doing that. One thing about the streets there is a code of loyalty and snitching was out of the question. We all went back and forth to court waiting to get a better offer, Skip and I wrote to each other from time to time and me and the lady were housed in the same unit.

Skip told me and the lady to cop out to the next offer which was two to four years because they were trying to slam him with a four to eight. He told us to go ahead and do what we needed to do and eventually we got sentenced to two to four years upstate and he copped out to four to eight years.

Chapter Seven

The Awakening

I didn't take the pleas of two to four years right away. I was struggling with the fact of having Skip take most of the blame and I couldn't understand why I was being convicted when I wasn't even the one that went into the store and stole the cigarettes. I was simply in the car. This is why it is important that we are careful of the company that we keep because you can be guilty by association, in the wrong place at the wrong time and thus, suffer major consequences for something you didn't do. I stayed in the county jail for as long as I could because many of the ladies that had been upstate before advised me of what I should do to be able to take my baby with me and to have as little time as possible upstate. During this time I reached out to Jerome and we began writing to each other. I was so happy that he was still doing well and serving the Lord with his whole heart. He had become a minister and was doing very well. I began to call Jerome on a regular basis and he would always speak about the Lord and Salvation to me. Each time I got off the phone with Jerome I felt stronger and encouraged. He told me to start to read my Bible consistently, He told me to just start by reading the book of John and keep reading and I did just as he said. I began to lock in my cell and read for hours and something was happening, I was changing. One day while I was reading; the Scripture jumped out at me and spoke to me. I had been going back and forth as to what I should do in regards to the plea that was offered to me. I would have to allow Skip to take the larger portion of the sentence. When there are co-defendants one person always gets the brink of the blame and the others get the deal. I knew that he had expressed to me to take the deal but I was struggling with that. I think because I was pregnant, he didn't want me to be in jail for so long. The Scripture that stood out to me on this particular day was John 8:32 "And ye shall know the truth, and the truth shall make you free."(KJV) It was like it came to life within me, I decided that I was going to simply be truthful in court and express exactly what happened and whatever happens, would happen and that's just what I did. I felt a burden lifted off of me and I got sentenced to two to four years upstate and I was okay with that. It was now the waiting game; I would stay downstate in riverhead as long as I possibly could before going upstate. I started going to church, Bible studies, women's groups, NA and AA, and personal counseling. Jerome was visiting and I spoke to him daily on the phone, we talked about the Bible and lots of other positive things. One of the things that helped me the most was I started to go to personal counseling while there. They had mental health counselors that you could see on a weekly basis. At first, I was just going to get off of the tier but there was something about this counselor, her name was Mrs. Mandarino. I really connected with her, she was easy to talk to and had a way of pulling out those things I needed to get out in a compassionate and nurturing way. I had been looking for this for so long and I had found it in a total stranger. I trusted her and was able to speak to her freely. She made me laugh, cry, forgive, heal and grow. She helped me bust through so many boundaries and walls I had set up over the years internally to block out traumatic events such as childhood hurt, sexual and mental abuse, addiction, rejection, abandonment, low self-esteem and so much more. She never judged me, or made me feel less than or ashamed about my mistakes and condition. This is something that is hard to find today. People today are judgmental and untrustworthy. This is something that is needed in order for people to be able to be vulnerable enough to express themselves so that healing can take place. I began to talk about the childhood issues that me and my mother went through. I expressed to her that I didn't know how to express to my mother what I felt throughout the years and so one of the exercises she gave me was I had to write a letter to my mother and tell her how I felt and how it affected me. This was a hard challenge for me to do and it was even harder for me to mail the letter to my mother because I was in fear of how she would respond to the letter. I understood that what I had to say may have hurt her, or put her through some feelings and the last thing I wanted to do was to cause her any pain but at the same time I needed to deal with my own issues. I mailed the letter and to my surprise my mother was able to respect my feelings, whether she thought they were right or wrong she showed genuine empathy and love and our healing process and new relationship began. Today, me and my mother are closer than we have ever been. Although there are times not often; but there are times when she will say something unintentionally and it will kick up old feelings but because of the intense counseling and the help of the Holy Spirit, I am able to process those feelings and move past them without them negatively taking root within me. I also dug in deep concerning all of the sexual abuse I went thorough being with different men for drugs and the multiple rapes I suffered which was hard to get through because once you get clean and sober you have to deal with the pain of all of your sufferings. I was at a crossroad in my life and I was determined to be healed from the inside out. I dealt with my abandonment issues, with not having a father figure in my life to be that protector that every daughter looks for in a dad. I also felt that I was cheated out of life because of my addiction, I missed out on my childhood, teenage years and being a young adult. I had a hard time understanding why I had to go through all that I went through from such a young age. Mrs. Mandarino and I worked through a lot and she was so patient with me I am forever grateful to her. I think about her often because she plays a major role in my transformation process. God will always bring people into your life for a divine moment in time to shift you from where you are into where you need to be, he knows exactly when you will be vulnerable enough to receive a Word of impartation. God always has a plan even in the midst of your mess. He is ready to make a way of escape for you, but He leaves us with the choice of choosing to take the way of life and not the road to destruction and death.

I was on a positive road even though I had to do a bid upstate. I was embracing it with a positive attitude because I was beginning to find myself, the real me. The old things were passing away little by little and all things were starting to become new within me. I began to love myself and the person I was becoming. It’s funny how someone or something can have a grip on you and power over your entire being. The drugs for so long had a grip on me and through an abusive relationship I relinquished my power and it was given to a man. It got so bad that I began to view myself as ugly and not worthy of anything greater than the life I had. All of that low mentality was dissipating. I was becoming strong, independent and confident. I was taking the power back.

I had regained my physical strength back, thank God I was healthy. I didn't catch any diseases or anything like that, my baby was healthy and strong. I was due to deliver a healthy baby boy before going upstate. I had gone to the doctor from my final appointment before my due date and the doctor checked me and everything was good. She said that I should be having the baby very soon and I was glad to hear the news. My due date came and went, I was now a day past my due date and it seemed like the baby was cozy and comfy inside my belly. It was a Thursday afternoon and I had been feeling the baby move and kick all that day just like every other day I was feeling good. It was 2:30pm and it was time for the jail to take a count of all the inmates. During the count everyone had to lock in their cell to be counted and stay locked in until the count is complete and confirmed. I went into my cell and I felt like I had to urinate, so when I went to go to the bathroom but instead of urine blood came pouring out into the toilet, something was seriously wrong. The blood came rushing out; as if someone turned on a water faucet full blast. I wasn't feeling any pain, I was feeling any movement I was just bleeding profusely. I screamed out to the ladies and they all began to scream for the guards. Once the guards came, they took me down to medical and I had to sit there in the medical office until someone came to transport me to the hospital. By the time they finally decided to come and get me to take me to the hospital there was blood all the way down past my knees and almost to the ankle of my pants. I got to the hospital and they threw me on a gurney and rushed me to the operating room. They had me sign a paper as they were rushing me down to the surgery room, they were checking for the baby's heartbeat. I was in a panic and didn't know what to think. I didn't know if the baby or if I was going to live or die. The next thing I remember was waking up handcuffed to my bed. I was in a lot of pain in my mid-section. They had to give me an emergency C-section. I was told that I almost died because I lost a severe amount of blood. I was given a blood transfusion during the surgery. No one was telling me anything about the baby, I knew from the silence that something was wrong but I didn't know for sure what it was. The doctors waited for a social worker to come into the room with them and then they informed me that my baby died. My baby was born stillborn. They explained to me that my placenta came off of the wall and when that happens the baby loses oxygen. The baby must be taken out within the first five minutes in order to survive and be healthy, anytime past five minutes the child would be brain dead if they survived.

I was in shock when they told me the news, I didn't even know what to feel. One part of me was sad but another part of me was at peace. The reason I say this is because I had bonded with the child during my pregnancy process but I was a bit relieved because I knew that I was about to go upstate for the next two to four years. It was better this way than having to see my baby off without me. They were talking to me about all these things I didn't want to discuss, things like naming the baby, and funeral arrangements. I didn't want to hear or deal with that. I reached out to my mother and she helped me by speaking to the social worker and they worked out with the funeral arrangements. It was heartbreaking for me. They brought my 7-pound deceased baby boy in the room wrapped up in a little receiving blanket and placed the baby in my arms. I broke down in tears, he was so handsome with a beautiful head of hair. After they let me hold him they took him away and later that evening they brought me a piece of his hair along with a picture of him and his footprints. I was so upset I was going back to my jail cell empty handed. I felt a void and didn't know how to fix the feelings I was feeling. If I were on the street I would have run and gotten high but I had to figure out a way to process the death of my baby. When I got back all of the ladies and the guards were so supportive which helped me get through the next few weeks of having to go to the funeral and burial. I was beginning to realize that I was able to handle and cope and get through adversities without the use of drugs.

The ladies on my tier were mostly ladies that were preparing to go upstate and I knew most of them from the streets or from being locked up with them in the past so we were all pretty close. We started what we called a church choir we would all gather together at a certain time in the evening and sing church songs, we read the Bible and prayed together as a group daily and it was very uplifting, we were all positively reinforcing one another preparing for our next destination, for some home and for others upstate.

I was getting positive support from the outside, Jerome and I were getting closer, and he was visiting me and uplifting me daily on the phone. My Aunt Geneva was a Christian and she was helping to support me while I was there. She said the Lord spoke to her and told her to send me money every week and she did faithfully. I could see the hand of God in the midst of my circumstance and I was trusting that his will would be done in my life. I did not know much in regards to the Bible but what I did know is that my faith in God was increasing and I was being compelled to read the Word and pray. Mentally I was prepared for my journey upstate and now I was waiting for my name to be called to roll up my stuff to go to my destination. I didn't know what to expect because I had heard so many different stories of what it is like upstate. Some of the stories were good and some bad.

Chapter Eight

Doing time Upstate

Minter Roll up! My name was called, it was early in the morning, somewhere around 4:00 am the girls woke up and bid me farewell. I quickly gave a few of my friends my stuff. You were not allowed to take anything with you except your Bible and paperwork. I was walked downstairs to the bullpen, there were two transport officers waiting for me there, they proceeded to handcuff my hands and shackle my feet, The handcuffs and shackles were different from what I was used to seeing, they had a black square piece that made sure you were not able to wiggle your way out of the cuff and shackles. They were a little more uncomfortable, especially having to wear them for such a long ride. I was going to Bedford Hills Correctional facility which was a few hours away in Westchester County. All ladies that were sentenced to a state bid had to go through Bedford Hills. You would either stay at Bedford which was a maximum-security facility, be sent from there to Albion Correctional facility which was further upstate and it is a medium security facility. Inmates that were doing time had an opportunity if they qualified to go to the Shock program. Now the shock program was for individuals going upstate for the first time. It was a six-month intense military-style boot camp that had strict discipline, physical exercise, military drills and ceremony upon graduation. One of the first things they did after you were physically cleared by the doctors was cut all of your hair off into a Caesar and once you were released you came home on shock parole which was a setup because it was almost impossible to succeed on shock parole. Most inmates that came home on shock parole violated and were sent back upstate to finish out their sentence. There was also a program similar to the shock program which was called Willard and this was for parole violators.

When I arrived there I was exhausted from the drive and the entire intake process. I was no longer acknowledged by my name but now a number. They immediately stripped my name and I was identified as 03G1190. I barely talked to anyone while I was in Bedford, we slept on bunk beds in a dorm room that was for the newcomers. I did meet a nice girl that was in the bunk next to me, we both had a top bunk so we talked a lot. She was like me. We stayed to ourselves and on our bunk reading our Bibles. You have to be careful who you speak to, who you looked at too hard because a lot of the women there had a wife and you didn't. It was the drama of a woman thinking that you were trying to push up and get with their wife. These women didn't play about their relationship, most of these ladies were in Bedford for a very long time and some were lifers and would beat you down or cut you up for getting in between their relationship. They didn't appear to be as friendly but I did come across some ladies that were nice. One good thing about being upstate is you were able to smoke cigarettes and the commissary was banging. They had all types of good food (Swanson fried chicken, rice, Aunt Jemima pancake mix, sausage, all kinds of cakes and candy, soda, coffee, creamer, canned food) a person could be content doing time upstate. Your clothing option was better, they had a beauty parlor where you could go and get your hair cut or permed, even the food in the mess hall was better. You worked while upstate and got paid, not a lot but it was something. The thing that was most impressive to me at Bedford was their church services. I decided to go to one of the church services with one of the ladies I met and when I walked in I couldn't believe how they were praising God. I sat down and was really in awe. I grew up Catholic and the church was never like this, they were singing and lifting up their hands, some were speaking in tongues and dancing, I could feel the presence of the Holy Spirit. I felt so good, something was happening to me. I began to cry. I wasn't sad and I didn't even know why I was crying but I was. I couldn't hold back the tears or this beautiful feeling I was feeling. I thought to myself "don't let them see you crying, they're going to think that you are scared" but something within me was stirring. I felt myself trembling and I was trying to fight the feeling I was feeling on the inside mainly because I didn't understand why I was feeling the way I did. I left the service feeling so good and I couldn't wait to call Jerome and tell him about what I experienced in the service. Jerome was and still is the one person in my life that gave me love and support in both the good times and in the bad times. He was a beacon of light for me and he gave me hope. It was good to know that I was not in this alone, that I had someone in my corner praying for me.

After about two weeks it was time to leave Bedford hills and the next stop was to the shock program. I was unsure if I wanted to do the program because I had heard so many different horror stories and how hard it would be. When I got there, I was assigned my sleeping area and sent to medical to see if I would be medically cleared to be a part of the program. The doctor performed a physical and I was not medically cleared because I had a Thyroid condition that caused me to have a lot of issues. I was diagnosed with Graves' disease a few years earlier and I was on medication for heart palpitations and to control my Thyroid. Graves' disease is an autoimmune disorder that causes the thyroid gland to produce too much thyroid hormone. The doctor felt that I was not a good candidate for the program due to me being on this medication and so I was to be transferred to Albion Correctional facility on the next bus leaving.

I stayed at the shock program for about three days and then I left for Albion. I was ready to get settled in one place, it was not easy having to keep going to a new place around new women. My anxiety was through the roof, having to adjust to each place. I desperately needed to be in one place so that I could adjust and wrap my brain around being wherever I was to do my time. Albion was very big and very busy with a lot of movement. It was very overwhelming. I can remember calling Jerome crying my eyes out and of course he always knew what to say to make me feel better. We laugh about it to this day, how I was shaken in my boots and crying for dear life that day on the phone. I stayed in one dorm for about three weeks and was then moved to another dorm that housed women in the drug program called Casat. I was friends with a girl named Razor. She was really nice and I had originally met her in Bedford hills and now she was here in Albion. For the first week or so I was going to the mess hall with her, smoking cigarettes together and getting to know each other. I thought to myself she's pretty cool. There was an older Spanish lady that slept directly across from me and I had gotten really close with her. She was teaching me all the ins and outs of who was who and which girls were in relationships so that I would be aware of not getting too friendly with someone's wife. She also made me aware that the girl Razor that I thought was nice and just being my friend wanted to be in a relationship with me. I was shocked, I didn't see that coming. I had to immediately stop hanging out with her because I was not trying to be involved in that way and I definitely didn't want her to misunderstand our friendship for something more. Thank God she was understanding. I simply told her that I liked her but not in that way and she was cool with that. I did stop hanging around her and we only spoke in passing from that point on. She was looking for a wife to pass her time and I was not. The older lady's name was Magaly. We became really good friends, she was like an older sister to me in there, and we looked out for each other. We shared food packages and cooked together. If I had then she had and if she had then I had. We went everywhere together, the yard, church, Bible studies, and choir rehearsal. Yes, we both joined the church choir, it was great. I loved the choir we would sing on Sundays during the church service, and we even had church choir robes. My eyes were opening spiritually in a place that I least expected. Jerome was writing to me on a regular basis, sending me spiritual books and I was praying a lot. The Lord was revealing himself to me in visions. My old way of thinking was changing. I was no longer thinking about who I left behind on the streets, I was no longer having drug dreams and anxious to get out to go back to the streets. My mindset was focused and sharp, I was determined to regain custody of my two boys Maliek and Kalief. While I was locked up my mother was unable to keep them any longer and they were sent to foster care. I was not mad at her because I understood that they were my children and my responsibility. She expressed how she could no longer manage caring for them and I had to be okay with that because if I was handling my responsibilities none of us would be in the predicament we were in. She had full custody of my daughter Shanikua since she was a few months old and that was all she could manage. I had purpose now, I wanted to come home and be a responsible mother, I wanted to serve the Lord with all my heart and be happy and whole. I was liking this person I had become and was determined to pursue what God had for me.

Now everyday was not a good day while I was there, there were days I felt depressed, saddened and discouraged but by the grace of God I pushed through those days. So much negativity was around me, people trying to sway you in the wrong direction, into drama and foolishness. Everybody that was incarcerated thought and acted differently, you had those that were in gangs, clicks, relationships, those that gossiped and caused drama and I had to make sure I stayed clear of all of that nonsense and stayed focused on what I was trying to accomplish for myself. I was trying to stay sane and stay out of harm's way.

You would hear of girls sleeping with the guards, one girl got pregnant from one of the guards. Another girl got Ajax and boiling water thrown in her face because she was trying to get with another girl's woman. I remember seeing that the young lady's face was messed up. It was red and bubbling up, it looked tremendously painful. She was screaming and holding her face. This was the moment I really realized that I had to be careful because these ladies didn't play around when it came to their significant other. I needed to stay clear from all of the drama because I was trying to make it home. I witnessed another girl getting her face cut wide open because she was pretty, the individual that cut her was jealous of her and saw her as a threat. I thank God that He had his angels dispatched round about me and that I had people on the outside interceding on my behalf. I know that it is because of prayer that I made it. The Bible says in James 5:16 "confess your faults one to another,and pray one for another, that ye may be healed,the effectual fervent prayer of a righteous man availeth much"(KJV) this was proving to be true I could feel the prayer being lifted up for me.

I had been at Albion for about twenty months and I received a letter from the Suffolk County family court in Central Islip, they were requesting that I appear in court because the family that had my boys wanted to adopt them. There was a law that if you are locked up for two years you could lose your parental rights. I was upset and was not trying to lose my children to the system. I was driven down-state to family court and the lawyer for the foster family and the children's law guardian began speaking about my past and how many times I had messed up before. I was feeling pretty bad and ashamed but my lawyer began to speak highly of me and all of the progress I had made since being incarcerated. I was working all of my programs, and having great success. I lifted up my head and I felt a fight rise up in me, I was not about to let these people take my children. The judge was also siding with me stating that it is not a light thing to just take away my parental rights regardless of what mistakes I had made in the past. The case was adjourned and I was taken back to Albion. I went back and began to pray to God asking him to favor me. I was about to go before the parole board soon and I desperately needed to get out if I didn't want to lose my parental rights. When I went before the parole board, they looked at my case and how I was doing while I was imprisoned. They asked me a bunch of questions about what I have learned and what I will do differently. I answered every question with honesty and to the best of my ability and trusted that the Lord's will would be done.

One evening during a mail call, they called my name, it was my determination letter from the parole board. I was nervous to open it because I didn't know what it was going to say. Prior to me receiving the letter some of the girls that had been locked up numerous times on parole violations expressed to me that if the envelope looked thick it was a denial but if it looked thin then it was approval to go home. I had my friend Magaly read the letter for me and to God be all the glory I was approved to go home from parole. I would finish out the rest of my sentence of two to four on parole. I had a release date which was about two weeks away from the day I received the letter. The first thing I did was call Jerome. I was so happy and so was he. After being released, I stayed at Jerome's house because I needed to be in a positive drug free environment and if I was going to get my life together, I needed to be around new places, people and things. He was the only real friend I had. He loved and cared for me and my wellbeing. Jerome and I were in a relationship by this point and He was the only real friend I had. He had proposed to me and I accepted. We laugh about that also because to his remembrance I was the one that proposed to him. But whichever way it went we were going to get married. I had to be careful for the next few weeks until my release date because it was told to me that oftentimes ladies that were there for a long time got envious and jealous because you received a release date. I know that God was working in my favor because the ladies told me that it was strange that I didn't get hit at the board because when you have a violent crime, they usually hit you at the board but one thing I have learned over the years that if God is on your side there is no closed door that he can't open. God was with me and if God be for me who can be against me. I stayed quiet and to myself for the next few weeks, I didn't talk about my release date I just prayed and waited patiently. When the day finally came, I was overjoyed but nervous at the same time. I had done so well behind prison doors but now the true test was about to happen. Would I pass or fail? Only God knew what the outcome would be, I surely didn't know. I gave away all of my things to my friend Magaly and told her that I would do my best to look out for her from the outside. I truly appreciated her friendship. The officers drove me to the bus stop, gave me my bus ticket and I headed to the bus terminal in the city.

Chapter 9

Restoration

Once I came home, I paroled at Jerome's house in Brentwood and began to do all that I needed to do in order to regain custody of my children. I knew that it was not going to be an easy journey but I was ready for the challenge. I was required to report to my parole officer immediately so the following day Jerome took me to the parole office. The parole officer's name was Mr. Johnson and he appeared to be a very nice man. He explained to me that I had a 9:00 pm curfew, I had to enroll in an outpatient drug program, anger management group, and family counseling for me and my boys and that he would be doing random house visits and urine drug tests. I was okay with all that was expected of me. I had only one request, I explained to him that I wanted to attend Bible studies and Friday night deliverance service and they ran later then my curfew. The Lord truly gave me favor because he didn't have a problem with me being out past my curfew as long as I was at a church function. Jerome reassured him that I would only be out past my curfew for church. Things were starting off well.

I started going to church with Jerome faithfully. I watched as the Holy Spirit moved on the people within the church and as they walked up to pay their tithes. They were all holding their envelopes proudly and with joy giving unto God. I thought to myself I want to do that. I didn't understand why they were doing it but I wanted to be a part of it. When I saw how the Holy Spirit was moving in and on them in each service, I wanted to feel what they felt. I remember one evening before I went to bed, I got on my knees and began to pray and one of the things I said was "God I want to feel what they are feeling in church" That was my prayer a simple prayer and because I was so grateful to God for what he was doing in my life my request would be answered sooner than I thought. The following Sunday I went to church and I sat in the front and listened attentively to the preached word of God. My Bishop at the time was preaching that Sunday morning and the Holy Spirit moved on the Word that morning and I was forever changed from that day. As the Word was being preached, I felt a consuming fire in my belly and I jumped up and began worshiping God, I couldn't control myself, I tried to sit down but I could not stop giving God praise, the tears were running down my face with unspeakable joy. I was filled with the Holy Ghost that morning. I didn't need a preacher to lay hands on me and I didn't have to do any type of theatrics. It was the unadulterated word of God that was preached with power and authority that moved on me that Sunday morning. I felt so alive and had such a reverence and gratitude for the Lord. I thought to myself how the Lord loved me so much that He would fill me with his precious spirit. I didn't feel that I deserved it but I was grateful that God did.

I was on a Spiritual high so to speak; I was running after Jesus. I lived and breathed church. I couldn't wait to go to church. It didn't matter what day, what time, how many services, how long the service was, or how I had to get to the church. If there was something going on at the church I needed to be there. Everything was going so well I was doing supervised visits with my boys and Shanikua was coming to the house for the weekend. My mother and I were getting along very well and Jerome and I had gotten engaged and I was working at an assisted living facility in Ronkonkoma. I loved my job, I loved working with the elderly. I have a soft spot for the seniors and so this job I enjoyed doing.

While at the job they were looking for new employees to work the housekeeping positions and I met a very nice woman named Nancy. She was from Brooklyn but had recently moved to Long Island with her Husband. Nancy and I became very close friends, she and her husband were in sobriety as well. We could relate to each other on a lot of things because our past was similar. The only difference was that in our sobriety she was staying clean by going to NA meetings and I was staying clean by going to church. Nancy and I are still friends today over twenty years now. Today, we serve the Lord together. It is hard to find real genuine friends that when push comes to shove, they are there for you no matter what and without any judgment. Nancy is one of those friends. At that time, we were really only friends through the job but she showed herself to be a true friend to me when I fell into trouble and the enemy almost dragged me all the way back into a life of destruction. When the Lord has called you with a purpose the enemy will not stop at trying to cause you to abort your assignment and ultimately kill you; even after you are saved. The warfare will get harder. Just when I thought things couldn't go wrong, they did. I felt like I could take on the world God was doing so many amazing things in me and I began to let my guard down. I was not yet spiritually strong, I didn't understand the attacks of the enemy, and I was still learning so much about staying saved, deliverance and applying the word of God to my daily life. The only thing I had experienced was God's love and the infilling of the Holy Spirit. I couldn't tell you how I got there but one day I found myself back in Bellport searching for drugs. I went to someone I used to know and they bought drugs for me. I started getting high. I now relapsed and was scared to go home. The Holy Spirit was convicting me and I was feeling tormented in my spirit.

I felt like the Apostle Paul when he said in Romans "I do not understand what I do. For what I want to do I do not do, but what I hate I do. And if I do what I do not want to do, I agree that the law is good. As it is, it is no longer myself who do it, but it is sin living in me. For I know that good itself does not dwell in me, that is, in my sinful nature. For I have the desire to do what is good, but I cannot carry it out. For I do not do the good I want to do, but the evil I do not want to do—this I keep on doing. Now if I do what I do not want to do, it is no longer I who do it, but it is sin living in me that does it." (Rom 7:15-20 NIV) Here I was back doing what I didn't want to be doing. I didn't understand why I would go back out to the streets all over again but something was calling me back out. I was listening to the voice of the enemy trying to pull me back into a life of destruction when God had already brought me out. Something was very different this time, I was different, I could not enjoy the high at all. Sitting in the spot with this drug dealer getting me as high as I wanted, there were plenty of drugs and everyone was enjoying themselves but me. Every time I took a hit I started talking about the Lord, I started to tell them about Jesus, I couldn't help it, that's all that was in me. Everyone was mad at me because I was blowing their high. I looked around at everyone and I heard the Holy Spirit say "daughter you no longer belong here." I thought to myself how I allowed myself to get here. I was feeling bad now thinking about what I had done and what I was going to do. The enemy was telling me "You can't go home, you messed up, they won't want to be bothered with you, just stay out here and keep on getting high." But down on the inside I knew that I had made a terrible mistake. I needed to be rescued quickly, fast and in a hurry. In the meantime, Jerome and my friend Nancy were out searching the streets of Bellport looking for me. Every spot they went to I had just left; the enemy did not want me to be found. This is what love is and does. When you love someone from the heart there is no length you aren't willing to go to save them. Jerome and Nancy exemplified the love of Christ. They dropped everything in order to find me because I was lost. The Scripture says in Matthew 18:12–14 "What do you think? If a man owns a hundred sheep, and one of them wanders away, will he not leave the ninety-nine on the hills and go to look for the one that wandered off? And if he finds it, truly I tell you, he is happier about that one sheep than about the ninety-nine that did not wander off"(KJV). In the same way your Father in heaven is not willing that any of these little ones should perish." I had wandered off and Jerome and Nancy were like the man in this passage of Scripture that left the ninety-nine and came after the one sheep that was lost. God used them to help steer me back home. They did not have any luck finding me that day but on the third day I was walking in the rain and I remember crying out to God, I was broken and extremely sorry for what I had done. I couldn't believe I had gone back out after the Lord touched me the way He did. I cried out and asked God if he would help me get out of this I would never look back and five minutes later a car pulled up beside me and it was Jerome. I was so happy and relieved to see him. God had answered my prayer right then and there, I knew it was God.

Jerome didn't say anything, he didn't scold me or judge me, we both just rode home quietly. When we got to the house I showered and laid down but something else was wrong with me, I was burning up with a fever and my body was weak. I was under spiritual attack, the enemy wasn't trying to let me go and I didn't recognize or understand that what was happening to me physically was a spiritual thing but Jerome knew. He grabbed the anointing oil and began to anoint me with the anointing oil. I mean he must have used a whole bottle and not a small bottle of oil you may receive from your pastor or at a conference. He was praying and calling out that spirit. I had never seen anyone pray the way he was praying that night. I laid there weak in my body; I could barely move. As he was rubbing me down with the oil and praying it felt like I could feel the spirit coming out of me. It's hard to explain but God was delivering me right there on the bed that night. From that night on I never looked back, I never went back, I never smoked crack ever again; this time I was free for real, freed by the power of Almighty God.

The next day was Sunday and I didnt want to go to church. I was ashamed that I had relapsed and went back to using drugs. I didn't want them to see me that way. The enemy will always try to trap you with feelings of shame in order to keep you from coming back to God. We went to church and to my surprise no one said anything, they didn't look at me funny or treat me any differently. They embraced me and showed me the love of God. They never said anything to me about what had happened even though they knew. What they did was love me back into the fold. The body of Christ gets this wrong in today's church. This is how we are to embrace those that were once lost but are now found. Embrace them with love and not with judgment. Don't look down on them or whisper about them behind their back for their shortcomings. It is our job to lift them up from where they have fallen and we do this by showing the love of Jesus Christ, the love that loves unconditionally.

Going to church that day was one of the hardest things I ever had to do. But I know today that if I had not gone to church that day and surrendered to God, I would not be serving the Lord the way I do today. The enemy likes to keep people bound to their sin and mistakes, and left up to him one would never turn back to God in repentance. So many people today make mistakes, fall short and forget that God is a loving and a kind God. He is a forgiving God and instead of people running to God when they mess up; they stay away from God as if God is not omniscient (All Knowing) and can't see what they are doing or have done behind clothes doors. Our Father knows all things and believers and nonbelievers alike run from God in their times of trouble; in those times they need to be rescued and freed from the bondage of sin.

For me the Lord forgave me and restored me and I put my past behind me from that day forward and have been running for my life ever since. The Lord delivered me and set me free and so I serve him with all my might. What Jesus did for me, no man gets the Glory. Jesus did what no program, prison, counselor, NA, AA could do. This is the reason why I serve him the way I do.

Jerome and I got married twenty years ago and during that time God did many things for me, He gave me favor with man. I have multiple felonies and I was told that I would never be able to work for certain jobs, in my case for a hospital because my felonies would stop me. When the Lord is on your side and moving in your life He can and will open every door that may be closed. God will bust the door down for you and give you divine access. The Lord restored my entire family. My daughter Shanikua came back to live with me when she was fourteen years old and my son Maliek when he was five years old and my other son Kalief was adopted when he was two years old by his foster parents. He was born autistic and it is not that I didn't love him but I had to make a very hard decision when I first came home from prison. At that time in my life, I did not feel that I was capable of caring for an autistic child and so I allowed the foster parents to adopt him with the stipulation that I was allowed to have visitation twice a year at their discretion. The visits never happened, no fault of my own, I guess they figured it wasn't best and I didn't push the issue. But God has a way of working all things together for your Good. The Scripture says in Romans 8:28 "And we know that all things work together for good to them that love God, to them who are called according to his purpose."(KJV) God worked the situation for my good in the end. When Kalief turned eighteen he began to search for his family. He found my son Maliek first and then we connected and he is now in our life once again. Although he is on his own God allowed us to have a relationship together as a family. The Lord blessed me with my youngest daughter Simone; my sobriety baby, I like to call her; God allowed me to experience all the joys of carrying and having a child in my new life of Salvation. I was able to do all the things a pregnant mother desires to do and experience during a pregnancy. While this may not seem like a big deal for some; it was a big deal for me. He brought restoration and healing to my relationship with my mother, blessed me with a husband that completes me. The Lord continues to open doors and bless me in ministry and in my personal life. The Lord has allowed me to excel in my education holding multiple degrees, started a not-for-profit organization called house of a Second Chance Transitional housing and pastor alongside my husband. Every day is not a good day I still have life's struggles and adversities like everyone else, I still have some personal struggles like everyone else, but I know that the hand of the Lord is on my life and that He called me for such a time as this to be a beacon of light to woman that feel like they can't make it out of the struggle they are in. Those struggles that they can't tell anyone about. God has called me to those women and I am committed to doing the will of the Father. Whatever the Lord tells me to do I will do, whenever He tells me to go, I will go. Any time I think about not doing something for the Lord I take a moment and roll back the curtains of time and remember all that the Lord has done for me.

Chapter Ten

The Flower

It was many years later that I heard the Lord speak to me in regards to sharing my story. I wasn't sure if this was something I wanted to do but the Lord said daughter it may not be what you want to do but it is what I have called you to do. Reluctant but obedient, I obeyed the voice of the Lord and wrote my story knowing that he has given me the stamp of approval and that if he has called me to share my story with others that it will make a positive impact in someone's life. I asked the Lord what is so special about my story, plenty of women have been through similar stories. He said to me because I know that you will be honest and that it will come from a pure place, not to get fame and glory, but to win a soul.

The Lord showed me that my life is like a flower, not just any flower but a specific flower. My life is like the flower that people look at as weeds, the type of flowers that people will walk over, step on or even try to pull up because they do not recognize the beauty that it will blossom into given the chance. He said you are like a hidden treasure; many see you and do see the beauty you have blossomed into because they never saw you in your past state, they haven't seen where I have brought you from, they only see the finished work and are basing it on your outer appearance. When a person looks at your life, daughter and how I have brought you out they will be able to see the true beauty that lies within you. God didn't compare my life to a rose or orchid that has beautiful petals and a sweet smelling fragrance. God told me that I was like a Dandelion, yes those flowers that we all look at and pull them up because they appear to be weeds. What we always fail to recognize about Dandelions is that they are resilient and have great strength and can outstand any storm. They push through concrete and even when they are pulled up or cut away they come back every year prepared to fight another battle. They are able to overcome adversity and are determined to blossom and live. When we look at the Dandelion we forget that this flower undergoes a beautiful and unique transformation. One that is different from any other flower. The Dandelion starts off as a yellow flower and it transforms into a fluffy puff with seeds at the bottom. I used to love these flowers when I was a kid, we would pick them and blow them until all the fluffy pieces were off of them. They were pretty and fun to play with at that stage of its transformation. Unfortunately, most people would pull them up before they were transformed to this stage. When they were yellow and in the beginning stages of their transformation they were looked upon as nothing but annoying weeds that are useless and good for nothing. Many people looked at me and thought that I also was useless and good for nothing simply because they were looking at me in the beginning stages of my life. What people did not realize is that God is the master builder and had a master plan for my life. Jeremiah 29:11 says "For I know the plans I have for you," declares the Lord, "plans to prosper you and not to harm you, plans to give you hope and a future." (NIV) I was one of God's creations; a unique and rare one of a kind vessel and he designed me so that he could get all the glory out of my life. He designed me with purpose. When God created me, he had a purpose in mind for everything that he created in me. Every living thing was created with a specific function and purpose in mind, this includes you and I. We are no different; there is a purpose for our creation and a purpose for our experiences. From the beginning of time the Lord designed the purpose for my life and he equipped me to accomplish what he called me to do. Jeremiah 1:5 says "Before I formed thee in the belly I knew thee; and before thou camest forth out of the womb I sanctified thee, and I ordained thee a prophet unto the nations."(KJV) All those years of darkness God was shaping me, molding me and causing me to be a woman of strength and resilience.

I understand today that God doesn't make any mistakes. My life may have started in a dark place and there was a process I had to go through, God allowed me to persevere through it all. The Lord used my circumstances to transform me into who I am today and I am grateful. Seeing the gifts within me during my time of suffering mentally I couldn't fathom it but today I can see the hand of God moving in my life all of those years. Just like the Dandelion flower the testimony of my life experiences represents hope, strength and resilience. We all have or will go through a process in life but the Lord God is with you, even in the darkest of times, even in those times you feel like he has left you but it says in Deuteronomy 31:6 "Be strong and courageous. Do not be afraid or terrified because of them, for the Lord your God goes with you; he will never leave you nor forsake you."(NIV) Regardless of what you have been through or what you are currently going through, be strong, be courageous, be resilient, fight your way through the darkness because the Lord is right there with you cheering you on. Jesus is interceding for you, he wants you to make it to your expected end. Jesus tells Peter in Luke 22:31-32 "And the Lord said, Simon, Simon, behold, Satan hath desired to have you, that he may sift you as wheat: But I have prayed for thee, that thy faith fail not: and when thou art converted, strengthen thy brethren."(KJV) I had to make up my mind that I would not let the enemy win in my life. Surrendering to Christ was the best decision I ever made. As I look back over my life I have been through much but I wouldn't change a thing because I understand that it made me who I am today.

The Dandelion is like all other flowers they attract pollinators. What I like about the Dandelion is this type of flower blooms early in the season and transforms to its fluffy state and as the winds blow it seeds blow far and wide allowing its plant seeds to disperse and reproduce effectively. While other flowers bloom later in the season, this flower's job has already been accomplished. Like this flower you and I have the capability to spread the Gospel far and wide; effectively to bring about more souls for the kingdom. We attract pollinators; many people attract pollinators; but once they attract them to themselves what fragrance are they giving off; is it one that smells like Jesus or some foreign smell. God had to process me so that when the wind (Holy Spirit) blew on me and sent me out to spread the Gospel those pollinators that attracted to me would see and smell Jesus and not a foreign smell. It is with an urgency that each of God's children allow the Lord to take them through their personal process so that each of us can spread the Gospel of Jesus Christ effectively and quickly.

I know that there will always be life challenges that I must face but as long as I face them with Christ Jesus I know for a fact that the outcome will work in my favor. I tried things on my own and the outcome was always the same: a world wind of destruction and so everything I do today I make sure I don't do it alone but I do it with Lord, He is the driver of my life, he knows the best way for me to take. It is my job to be an obedient passenger and let Jesus take me to my destiny. This is not always easy for me to do, oftentimes I find myself trying to grab the steering wheel, or tell the Lord I think we should go right instead of left or to stop. There are times when he is telling me to go forward and I am hesitant because trusting God can be challenging at times. But I continue to grow daily and submit daily to the will of God for my life. I simply want to hear him say *"well done my good and faithful servant."* It is my desire to do all that I can, while I can to glorify the name of the Lord. He is truly my Savior, and my Deliver and to him I owe my life.

The Lord delivered me from a life of drug addiction and abuse twenty years ago and my life today speaks of the power of God being exemplified in someone's life. We still serve the same God, the God that had the power to save and deliver me can save and deliver you to. The Bible says in Hebrews 13:8 "Jesus Christ the same yesterday, and today, and forever."(KJV) All one has to do to begin their process of healing is accept Jesus Christ as their Lord and Savior it's that simple! Romans 10:9 "that if you confess with your mouth the Lord Jesus and believe in your heart that God has raised Him from the dead, you will be saved."(NKJV) Salvation is free and available to everyone no matter how far in the gutter one may think that they are. Jesus is waiting for you with his arms open wide ready to receive you. Jesus has been knocking at the door of your heart for a long time now. Will you let him in today? Revelation 3:20 says "Behold, I stand at the door, and knock: if any man hears my voice, and opens the door, I will come in to him, and will sup with him, and he with me." Jesus is knocking!(KJV)

I hope that this book has encouraged someone to know that no matter what you are going through, the Lord can bring you out and set you free.

If you feel led to give your life to Jesus Christ our Lord and Savior and soon coming King. You can recite the sinners' prayer below. Knowing that one accepts Christ as their Lord and Savior, the Bible says that the host of angels in heaven rejoice over your soul being saved. Luke 15:10 "In the same way, I tell you, there is rejoicing in the presence of the angels of God over one sinner who repents."(NIV)

Prayer for repentance and Salvation

Heavenly Father I come to you in prayer asking for forgiveness of my sins, I confess with my mouth today and believe in my heart that you are Lord and that you Jesus died on the cross for my sins and was risen on the third day and now you are seated and the right hand of the Father making intercession for me. I ask that you wash me and cleanse me; come into my heart and dwell there. I accept you today as my Lord and Savior In Jesus Name I pray Amen.

Made in the USA
Middletown, DE
09 November 2024

64083554R00076